Management for Professionals

The Springer series "Management for Professionals" comprises high-level business and management books for executives, MBA students, and practice-oriented business researchers. The topics cover all themes relevant to businesses and the business ecosystem. The authors are experienced business professionals and renowned professors who combine scientific backgrounds, best practices, and entrepreneurial vision to provide powerful insights into achieving business excellence.

The Series is SCOPUS-indexed.

Christos Voudouris

Autonomic Business Transformation

A Guide to AI Agents for Practitioners and Executives

Springer

Christos Voudouris
Reading, UK

ISSN 2192-8096 ISSN 2192-810X (electronic)
Management for Professionals
ISBN 978-3-032-01414-6 ISBN 978-3-032-01415-3 (eBook)
https://doi.org/10.1007/978-3-032-01415-3

This Springer imprint is published by the registered company Springer Nature Switzerland AG
The registered company address is: Gewerbestrasse 11, 6330 Cham, Switzerland

To my family for your love and encouragement and to my teachers and mentors for your patience, guidance, and unwavering belief in my potential.

Preface

This book offers an overview of the emerging area of autonomic business. A key differentiating feature of autonomic business compared to digital business is that AI becomes the primary driver of automation within an organization. With digital business gradually giving way to autonomic business, there is a need to transition the conversation and address the new opportunities and challenges a plethora of new AI technologies are beginning to present to the enterprise.

Executive leaders will be tasked with understanding and leading changes in the AI era. However, it is becoming increasingly difficult for them to grasp the details of what AI means in a business context. Even more so, it is harder to foresee what will take place in the next few years as the AI wave ushers in a new era of unprecedented automation for organizations. This book provides insight into this future and the actions and plans organizations can put in motion *today* to start their AI transformation journey.

With over 20 years of R&D in AI applications, followed by executive business roles in key global technology and analyst organizations, the author of the book clearly lays out the vision of an AI-driven business where intelligent agents take charge of processes and systems (assuming the role of the 'pilot' rather than the 'co-pilot'). This bold vision and idea is not new. It actually dates to the mid-1990s, if not earlier, when visionaries in the domain of multi-agent systems started working on AI prototypes validating the concept of AI-driven autonomous operations and value chains.

It took another 30 years for the technologies to develop and fuse to make that vision a reality. Big leaps along the way included realizing an interconnected and mobile world, followed by digital, data, and cloud technologies taking centre stage and reaching global scale. This allowed a new generation of algorithms to learn the patterns of human intelligence by digesting vast amounts of data, achieving incredible powers along the way in cognition, natural language understanding, and decision-making, beyond what was thought possible only a few years ago.

The era of autonomic business, partly or largely run by intelligent agents, is now on the cusp of becoming a reality. It is the firm belief of the author that autonomic business is not about machines dictating what humans do, but rather executing processes and tasks on our behalf, gradually reducing the degree of attention and effort we need to expend to achieve our goals and objectives, hence the notion of autonomic systems instead of fully autonomous ones.

This book provides the necessary tools and frameworks to understand this change and allow business and technology leaders to execute an autonomic business vision while controlling risks and managing expectations. Change is never easy, and even more so when it entails giving systems increasing levels of autonomy to achieve goals on our behalf. However, change is often inevitable, and this is where this book puts the reader centre stage and in the driving seat, ready for the AI era.

Reading, UK Christos Voudouris

Acknowledgements

Bringing this book to realisation has been a journey that lasted over 30 years and has been shaped by many individuals whose encouragement, insights, and collaboration led to the many projects and ideas on AI and autonomous agents.

In this latest endeavour, I would like to thank Felix Torres Serrano for his editorial guidance, interest in AI, and encouragement but also patience to bring to life a book on such a rapidly evolving and ambitious topic. Your support has been invaluable in shaping this work and bringing it to a successful conclusion. My sincere thanks also go to Springer Nature for providing a platform for sharing pioneering ideas that may shape the future of business for years to come.

I am especially grateful to Arun Chandrasekaran, Don Scheibenreif, and Marc Kerremans, former colleagues whose work on AI trends, machine customers, and business automation is truly pioneering. They provided inspiration and feedback, further affirming my belief that the topic of Autonomic Business and AI agents explored in this book has now reached maturity and is of broader interest and relevance to a wider business audience.

Likewise, I owe much to the AI team at the National and Kapodistrian University of Athens, and in particular to Prof. Manolis Koubarakis for his leadership and to Myrto Tsokanaridou for engaging in thoughtful and stimulating exchanges on the topics of AI agents and Multi-Agent Systems and how these can be translated into real systems for business applications.

To my former colleagues at BT Labs, Nader Azarmi, Paul O'Brien, Simon Thompson, and Gilbert Owusu, thank you for collaborating with me on exciting and challenging AI and autonomous agent projects over the years.

I am indebted to my long-time academic collaborator, Prof. Edward Tsang, for involving me into the work of the Centre for Computational Finance and Economic Agents (CCFEA) at the University of Essex and the application of AI agents in financial markets.

To the many colleagues and team members over the years who contributed to turning theory into AI toolkits and systems that allowed us to experiment with agentic, robotic and other AI technologies years ahead of their becoming mainstream, thank you.

These early works on AI technologies would not have been possible without research funding from government bodies in the UK and EU, whose foresight and commitment enabled ambitious AI research long before the field drew broader attention.

Finally, to my family and close friends, thank you for your unwavering patience, encouragement, and support.

Last but not least, to the readers of this book, I hope the ideas within it inspire thought leadership in real businesses for years to come.

Competing Interests The author has no competing interests to declare that are relevant to the content of this manuscript.

Contents

List of Abbreviations

AB	Autonomic Business
ABOS	Autonomic Business Operating System
ACL	Agent Communication Language
ACP	Agent Communication Protocol
AI	Artificial Intelligence
AOC	Autonomic Operations Centre
API	Application Programming Interface
ASIC	Application-Specific Integrated Circuit
BPM	Business Process Management
CBR	Case-Based Reasoning
CCO	Chief Commercial Officer
CDAO	Chief Digital and Analytics Officer
CDO	Chief Digital Officer
CEA	Chief Enterprise Architect
CEO	Chief Executive Officer
CIO	Chief Information Officer
CLP	Constraint Logic Programming
CMO	Chief Marketing Officer
COO	Chief Operations Officer
CoT	Chain of Thought
CRM	Customer Relationship Management
CTO	Chief Technology Officer
D&A	Data and Analytics
DT	Digital Twin
DTO	Digital Twin of the Organization
ERP	Enterprise Resource Planning
FLOPS	Floating-point Operations Per Second
GPU	Graphics Processing Unit
LAM	Large Action Model
LCM	Large Cognitive Model
LLM	Large Language Model

LMM	Large Multimodal Model
LP	Logic Programming
LRM	Large Reasoning Model
MAS	Multi-Agent System
MCP	Model Context Protocol
ML	Machine Learning
MRP	Material Requirements Planning
NPS	Net Promoter Score
OCR	Optical Character Recognition
OLA	Operational-Level Agreement
RL	Reinforcement Learning
RPA	Robotic Process Automation
SLM	Small Language Model
SCM	Supply Chain Management
SLA	Service Level Agreement
ToT	Tree of Thought
UI	User Interface
UX	User Experience

Chapter 1
Digital Business to Autonomic Business

Technological change has been unprecedented in the past 30 years, driven by innovation in information systems, telecommunication services, and electronics, all combining to deliver wave after wave of business transformation. Technological change is in some ways irrevocably linked to business transformation and vice

C. Voudouris, *Autonomic Business Transformation*, Management for Professionals, https://doi.org/10.1007/978-3-032-01415-3_1

versa, with disruptive technologies fuelling business innovation, which in turn provides the funding and resources for the next wave of technological advancements to take place.

This continuous interplay between technology and business change has manifested itself into discrete and clearly identifiable periods or eras defined by certain technologies becoming enablers for new ways of doing business. In each of these eras, it was not always clear upfront what business and operating model changes were needed to take full advantage of the new technologies, often leading to a steep learning curve based more on a trial-and-error approach rather than a systematic way of leveraging new technologies and deploying them to maximum effect. As we are about to embark on the next wave of business transformation based on AI technologies, this book aims to provide a comprehensive guide on the changes to be expected and what practical steps organizations can take to prepare so that they can thrive rather than merely survive.

This upcoming wave of technological change is profoundly different from all the previous ones in that AI introduces the notion of autonomy for machines to decide and act to levels unparalleled compared to historical precedents, with ever-diminishing human input and supervision required. A clear distinction to make here is whether AI systems to be considered will be self-governing or self-managing. It could be argued that AI setting its own rules and governance may be some years away, and it is probably the case if one considers the whole enterprise with its board and CEO, where business governance cannot possibly be transferred to a machine setting the company strategy and allocating resources accordingly to achieve its goals. In that sense, it is more reasonable to consider the notion of self-managing systems that can serve their purpose, delivering the desired business outcomes in a limited context largely on their own, ideally minimizing human effort to steer the technologies towards the desired goals and outcomes.

We are not saying something groundbreaking here, but as humans, we rather prefer AI to be working more like our 'gut' rather than our 'brain' at least in the short to medium term until we build the necessary trust in the reasoning and planning abilities of the emerging AI solutions. Perhaps a better word to describe such technology is 'autonomic' rather than 'autonomous', which, similarly to our 'autonomic nervous system', takes care of key functions for us with limited attention in a self-managing and self-adaptive fashion rather than dictating our goals and actions.

In fact, one may consider an autonomic scale ranging from the pure and simple automation you find in a thermostat to the fully autonomous cars driving you to your destination or domestic robots of the future taking care of home chores all without requiring constant input and supervision.

This brings us to the title of the book, which is *Autonomic Business Transformation*. The aim is to capture the range of possible outcomes we can expect from applying AI-based self-managing technologies and systems to transform a business across the full spectrum from simple forms of automation all the way to autonomous systems and in-between. Before we delve into the topic, we explore a few definitions that can clarify the concepts and define the scope of this work as well as provide a historical perspective on how the topic has developed.

1.1 Defining AI Agents

We are clearly entering a period of change driven by AI technologies. This follows a long era defined by digital technologies and the adoption of digital business. While the work on digital transformation is not yet complete, we are undoubtedly entering a new period or era that can be considered the 'post-digital' business era [1].

One key defining feature of this emerging period is the increased ability of systems equipped with AI capabilities to operate with partial or full autonomy, executing tasks on behalf of their users. This is not a completely new idea, as automation is a well-known and understood concept in engineering, examined under disciplines such as control theory [2], which dates to the nineteenth century. However, the degree of anthropomorphic capabilities exhibited by AI-based systems is now reaching such a level that automating human tasks requiring certain levels of intelligence can now be considered within reach [3].

Thus, a key enabler of this upcoming period is the introduction and adoption of these AI-enhanced, partially or fully autonomous systems across all spheres of life, including their business applications. Several definitions exist to capture these systems, starting with Autonomic Computing introduced by IBM [4]. In their definition, Autonomic Computing is the self-managing approach to computing in which systems can automatically configure, optimize, and heal themselves. This term has been further developed by Gartner, which also defined autonomic systems and included them in their 2022 Top Technology Trends report [5]. According to Gartner, autonomic systems are self-managing physical or software systems, performing domain-bounded tasks, which exhibit three fundamental characteristics:

Autonomy: Execute their own decisions and tasks autonomously without external assistance.

Adaptivity: Modify their behaviour and internal operations based on experience, changing conditions, or goals.

Agency: Have a sense of their own internal state and purpose that guides how and what they learn and enables them to act independently.

These definitions start to paint the picture of the key attributes of the upcoming period, with properties such as self-managing, self-healing, autonomy, continuous learning, and agency characterizing both physical and software technological innovations enabled by AI. One term that seems to encapsulate all these properties and is increasingly used to refer to these systems is *AI agents*, with the overall systems which includes orchestration and governance referred to as *agentic AI*. We will use the term AI agents throughout this book to refer to autonomic systems underpinned by autonomic computing. There is no clear consensus on a definition, but AI agents have a strong link to autonomous agents [6] and agent-based computing [7].

Autonomy and agency are interlinked concepts but not identical. According to the Cambridge English Dictionary, *agency* is defined as the ability to take action or to choose what action to take [8], while *autonomy* is the ability to make your own decisions without being controlled by someone else [9]. For AI agents to be transformational in a business context, they need to exhibit both autonomy and agency to a certain degree so that, given a goal, they can make decisions on how to best achieve it, have the capacity to act on these decisions, and choose which actions are best to take. Although necessary, autonomy and agency are not sufficient characteristics. To successfully operate, AI agents would also require sufficient computational ability to model their complex environments, allowing them to modify their behaviour to reach a set goal or meet certain performance criteria. This brings the notion of adaptivity as the third pillar for AI agents, which is essentially no different from adaptive control or learning control in traditional control systems theory [10]. To summarize (→ Fig. 1.1), Autonomy, Agency, and Adaptivity (Triple-A) are three key defining characteristics of AI agents as considered in this book. Providing clarity on these aspects can help the domain maintain its integrity and avoid gradual dilution.

Overhyping AI agents and trivializing the term to refer to anything that uses AI will only raise false expectations and hinder true business value realization. There has been tremendous enthusiasm for AI agents since late 2024, continuing unabated in 2025. Prominent technology leaders such as Marc Benioff of Salesforce [11], Satya Nadella of Microsoft [12], and Sam Altman of OpenAI [13] have all proclaimed that AI agents will soon join the workforce as digital labour. However, with tech companies and their marketing departments entering the fray, it is unlikely that views will converge around one agreed definition soon, as each company will try to align the concept with its own capabilities and plans.

The current spectrum of uses for the term AI agents varies from enhanced chatbots and AI assistants to general AI systems interacting with humans and performing tasks, to new apps powered by AI offering domain-specific expertise. Similarly, any software incorporating aspects of generative AI [14], a key technology in the current AI wave, is often labelled as agentic, adding to the overall confusion.

Using the three defining characteristics of Autonomy, Agency, and Adaptivity can help us distinguish between genuine agentic systems versus more traditional

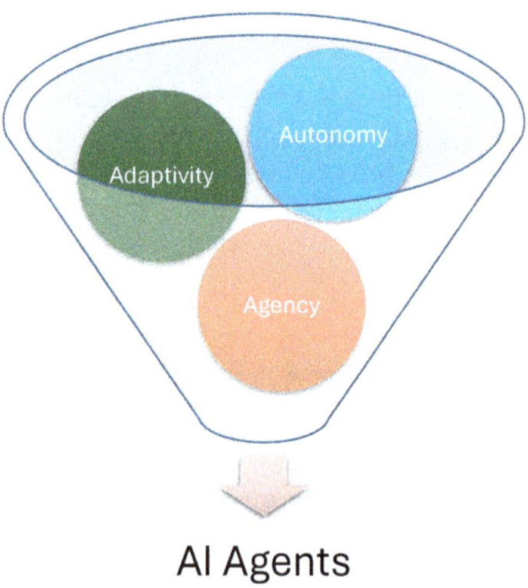

Fig. 1.1 Autonomy, Agency, and Adaptivity are three defining AI agent characteristics

customer service or transactional application software rebadged as agentic by marketing departments.

1.2 Defining Autonomic Business

Turning now to the business application of AI agents, one can consider them to perform several activities within a business context, from executing individual tasks to coordinating processes to delivering or procuring products and services. They can interact with humans, IT systems, or even other AI agents to achieve their goals. This goes beyond traditional approaches such as business process management (BPM) [15] or robotic process automation (RPA) [16], introducing concepts such as autonomic business operations [17] and, more broadly, the overall concept of autonomic business.

We define *autonomic business* (or AB for short) as the form of business where AI agents, exhibiting their key defining characteristics of Autonomy, Agency, and Adaptivity to varying degrees, are deployed within an organization to achieve its business strategy and enterprise objectives. Autonomic businesses have the ability to learn, configure, and optimize themselves and generally respond in a self-managing fashion to changing internal and external conditions.

In our definition, *Enterprise Governance* as described by the likes of IBM [18], i.e. aligning strategic objectives to processes and resources, is largely still human-driven, hence the use of the term 'autonomic'. If an enterprise in the future is also partly or fully governed by AI agents, it may be characterized as a fully or partly 'autonomous' business. However, it is unlikely that in the short to medium term, or even in the long term, businesses will abolish roles like the CEO or abandon corporate governance and delegate all that to AI agents, even if they attain full Triple-A capabilities comparable to human levels. This may not be a decision necessarily dictated by the capabilities of the technologies but perhaps due to law and regulation, at least as they stand for the foreseeable future, whereas they mandate that companies be managed by human directors and officers who bear fiduciary duties and legal responsibilities (e.g. see [19]).

1.3 Waves of Technology: A Historical Perspective

A historical perspective on how we arrived at the beginning of this new period or era with the emergence of AI agents giving rise to autonomic business can provide additional insight and understanding. One way to describe different eras is through the concept of industrial revolutions [20]. Some may argue whether Industry 4.0 or 5.0 captures the essence of autonomic business. In our view, Industry 4.0 [21] and 5.0 [22] are broader in scope and perhaps more relevant to a European and rather manufacturing audience, as these themes originate from the original industrial revolution itself.

Autonomic business is narrower and specifically focused on the changes to the business and operating models of organizations as they are impacted by technological developments. The wider implications for society and humanity could be better captured by these other terms and definitions of the era we live in.

Considering this narrow business and operating model view, one may identify some discrete periods or eras enabled by specific technological advancements. We list these in Table 1.1.

One interesting observation from glancing at the table is the spread of the impact from ICT technologies, starting from the back office and operations, moving through to the front office, and culminating in the digitization of end products and services, which brings us to our current time. The autonomic business enables the creation of a whole machine-driven layer within and across organizations, with varying degrees of autonomy and self-managing capabilities, sitting below the human interaction layer and acting on its behalf. This avenue is explored further with regard to machine customers in a recent book by Scheibenreif and Raskino [23].

It is interesting to note that most technological eras span around a decade and a half without showing significant acceleration between one era and the next, at least up to now. This seems to be constrained by the ability to productize, introduce, and absorb new technologies within organizations and from the vendor community as well as develop new technologies that will fuel the next wave. If the pattern is repeated, then this will be despite the substantial funding allocated in AI such as the investment in generative AI and foundation models by the digital giants. These investments are currently further fuelled by increased venture capital investment in AI agent startups as well as public funding support for AI as it is the case in Europe [24]. For example, according to CB Insights [25], investment in AI agents reached \$980 M in 2024 up to July, almost double the amount for the entire previous year, 2023.

A recently compiled AI agent index capturing commercially deployed or open-source projects [26] shows that AI agent deployments are accelerating, with half of all systems in the index deployed in the second half of 2024. Most of these

Table 1.1 Evolution of business eras and their technological drivers

Period/Era	Dates	Rapidly growing technologies	Main impact areas	Key change
IT-enabled business	1990s—2000s	ERP, CRM, MRP, SCM, 2G / ISDN	Back office, operations	Improved operations through the use of IT
Electronic business	2000s—2010s	Internet, web, mobile, 3G / ADSL	Front office	New ways of selling through web and mobile
Digital business	2010s—2020s	Cloud, IoT, data and analytics, APIs, 4G / VDSL	Product and services	New digital products and services
Autonomic business	2020s—2030s	AI, LLMs, AI agents, 5G / fibre	All	New machine layer within and across organizations

deployments are from US companies, with big companies representing nearly three-quarters of the deployments. The focus so far has been primarily on software engineering and computer automation. This suggests that, at least in the current growth phase, the emphasis is on automating structured tasks such as coding or navigating interfaces, rather than more challenging problem-solving and reasoning that someone may have expected given the increased hype on AI's abilities.

However, this does not seem to sap enthusiasm in the industry. In another report by Deloitte [27], it is predicted that 25% of companies using generative AI will proceed to POCs of agentic AI in 2025, with the figure growing to 50% by 2027. Some use cases in certain industries may see actual adoption into existing workflows in 2025, especially by the second half of the year.

An even more optimistic assessment is provided by Boston Consulting Group [28], which projects that the market for AI agents will grow at a 45% CAGR, reaching $52.1 billion by 2030 from $5.7 billion in 2024. One may wonder what is fueling this optimism and where do we go from here.

1.4 How AI Agents Impact the Business Model

Fundamental to the impact of any technological wave, and its promise for adoption is its effect on the business model, which is the heart of the business where value is generated. In the previous section, we considered autonomic business, encompassing the impact of AI agents on all aspects of the business, in contrast to previous waves that tended to have a more focused impact on operations, back office, or products and services. To demonstrate this further, we consider the simple concept of the business model canvas, a tool typically used by venture capitalists when evaluating new businesses [29]. The business model canvas captures the following areas, each with its unique potential to be disrupted by AI agents. These are merely examples in each category and the list is also not exhaustive in terms of potential impact areas:

Customer segments: New AI agent customers procuring services on behalf of others.

Value propositions: New services targeted at AI agents representing customers.

Channels: Selling through and to AI agents.

Customer relationships: Connecting to customers through agentic experiences and interfaces.

Revenue streams: New revenue streams through sales to AI agents.

Key resources: Digital workers implemented as AI agents.

Key activities: Autonomic business operations with AI agents orchestrating processes and executing tasks.

Key partners: New agentic ecosystems supporting dynamic service composition through multi-agent collaboration.

Cost structure: Relying on AI-based automation to optimize operational costs and dynamically adapt to demand fluctuations.

By looking at the above list, one can easily see that AI agents can add a machine-driven dimension to all these areas, which is a testament to the far-reaching impact an autonomic business model may have compared to a traditional one. The potential of AI agents across a business model can be truly transformational. We will analyse how to tap into this transformation throughout this book and how practitioners and executives can prepare for this upcoming business model evolution or, as some may say, revolution.

AI agents have a range of applications from personal assistants under the control of individuals all the way to enterprise software executing autonomously business workflows. In this book, we focus on the latter rather than the former since we strongly believe the more structured enterprise environment is a fertile area for this technological revolution to reap its early benefits. The idea of applying AI agents to business workflows is not new so we examine its origins below and how we arrived at this latest inflection point.

1.5 Origins of Autonomic Business and Why Now

Autonomic business has its origins in the mid-1990s and even earlier when multi-agent systems (MAS) [30] were applied in the context of business process automation, with standards developed by academia and industry (e.g. IEEE FIPA—Foundation for Intelligent Physical Agents [31]) on how these systems can interoperate within and across organizations. The author of this book worked on this topic as far back as 1995, developing prototype systems for managing business processes using AI agents for projects sponsored by the UK and the EU. One notable project sponsored by UK's Department of Trade and Industry, called ADEPT [32–34], explored the specific use of agents in fully automating end-to-end business processes, ultimately winning the British Computer Society's IT Award for Innovation in 1997 [35].

One of the key concepts pursued at the time was the notion of agent-based computing as an alternative way of architecting systems [36, 37], utilizing two fundamental principles:

Decomposing the overall system functionality into functional modules that can be implemented and managed by individual AI agents.

Developing a standardized architecture for the capabilities of agents to encompass coordination, reasoning, planning and scheduling, task execution, etc.

The R&D community invested in the topic, organized efforts to formulate agent standards, and developed toolkits to support agent-based computing. This came in the form of the FIPA organization [31] under the auspices of IEEE and the development of communication languages for agents, such as the Agent Communication Language [38]. Telecommunication companies were particularly interested at the time, devoting significant funding in agent toolkit development, most notably Telecom Italia with their open-source JADE platform [39] and BT with their ZEUS toolkit [40], which was later also open-sourced [41].

The concepts were quite advanced for their time, even advocating the use of autonomous agents operating across businesses with little or no human intervention. EU-funded R&D activities, such as the AgentCities.RTD program [42], explored this later concept. The author of this book even conceived a project on Generative Software Development [43, 44] together with UCL and Prof. Anthony Finkelstein, which now seems like a good idea to pursue but was clearly ahead of its time back in the mid-2000s. With renewed interest in AI agents, these early concepts of agent-based ecosystems cannot be excluded in the near future, nor the idea of self-generating agentic technologies. We will discuss agentic ecosystems later in this book and explore its potential applications.

The author having worked on or managed some of these advanced projects such as ADEPT [32], ZEUS [41], AgentCities.RTD [42], and topics on Generative Software Development [43] during his time at BT Labs was genuinely intrigued as to what motivated large organizations, especially in the telecom sector, to invest so heavily in these nascent technologies. Although anecdotal, one big concern at the time was that the digital operation of the network (e.g. through the introduction of the digital switching System X [45]) would eventually lead to insurmountable management issues for classic software architectures based on object-oriented programming. This would have required agent-oriented programming and the automation of software development to make things work.

Of course, at the time, this was not proven to be the case with IP networks able to scale globally. Interest eventually waned on autonomous agent-managed networks even among the most committed R&D teams especially as the focus shifted to Internet, web, and mobile innovations that started to gain momentum around the same time. Although some work continued in exploring use cases for AI agents, such as addressing distributed resource allocation [46] or empowering workers through personal agents [47], the broader vision of an autonomous, AI-driven network was ultimately set aside. Remarkably, nearly 30 years later, that vision is now on the cusp of becoming a reality (see Sect. 5.5). So, what changed to bring the spotlight back to autonomic business and the potential of AI agents in telecoms but also in so many other domains?

Early agentic approaches primarily relied on rule-based systems and symbolic AI for reasoning, necessitating the creation of specific communication languages and domain ontologies. This complexity limited their widespread adoption and practical application. However, the advent of generative AI [14] and large language models (LLMs) [48] has significantly enhanced AI agent capabilities, paving the way for the realization of autonomic business. This new generation of agents possesses a flexible and powerful 'brain' capable of navigating real-world uncertainties and communicating in natural language.

Moreover, emerging protocols such as the Model Context Protocol (MCP) by Anthropic [49] and the Agent2Agent protocol by Google [50] (see Sect. 3.2.3) enable these agents to access tools, data, and information, as well as exchange context information. These advancements allow agents to operate effectively in diverse IT and software environments. The integration of natural language and machine data capabilities further enhances their flexibility, making them valuable tools, co-pilots, or companions for regular employees in human-dominated, IT-driven business environments, rather than specialized software tools limited to a few technology experts as it was the case in the past.

1.5.1 What Comes After Autonomic Business: X-Verses and the Rise of Quantum Computing

Before we delve deeper into AI agents and autonomic business, one might wonder what could follow as the next era. Predicting the future has always been challenging, as it often hinges on the convergence of multiple technologies to create the next wave. Based on our current understanding of emerging technologies and technology trends, we can anticipate that quantum computing [51], Artificial General Intelligence (AGI) [52, 53], and 6G communication technologies [54] will play significant roles. Additionally, a more advanced version of the Metaverse [55], which has yet to fully materialize, may also contribute.

Given the emerging layers of interaction between machines and humans, it is plausible to envision the rise of several digital spaces, or X-verses. These could be machine-driven, human-driven, or hybrid environments where humans and machines interact seamlessly across digital and physical realms. We expect this X-Verse Business to emerge sometime in the 2030s. In many ways, it may deliver some of the experiences envisioned by the Metaverse, but with a stronger emphasis on AI and supported by a highly advanced computational infrastructure that blends virtual realities with the physical world. These realities will be powered by 6G communications utilizing Terahertz spectrum, with fibre networks and cloud computing infrastructure tightly integrated through new approaches such as optical computing [56].

Figure 1.2 illustrates this projected period, extending from autonomic business to what might come next.

One key technology trend likely to underpin this advanced computational infrastructure is quantum computing. To develop the digital worlds of the future, we will need to harness the principles of quantum mechanics that govern the real world.

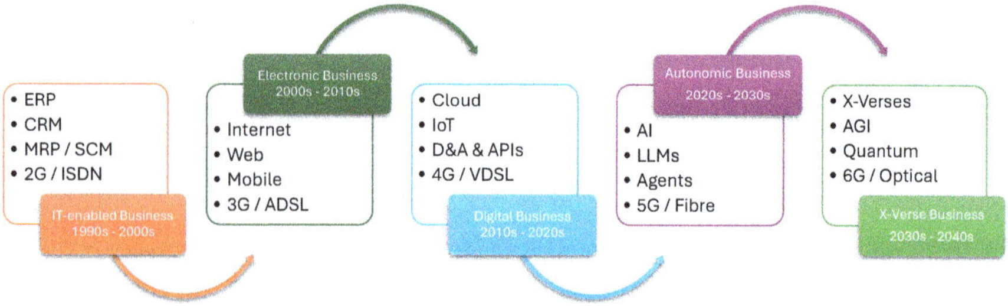

Fig. 1.2 The business eras and associated technological advancements

Despite being identified as a promising technology for years, quantum computing has yet to make the predicted impact. This is not uncommon for breakthrough technologies, as AI itself experienced several cycles of excitement and disillusionment before reaching its current state. A critical challenge for quantum computing is identifying and tackling the specific computational tasks central to AI and machine learning, so that the training and execution of even larger models can be significantly accelerated [57, 58]. Achieving this could make currently intractable problems solvable.

Figure 1.3 depicts a potential technology stack of the future as discussed in this section.

1.5.2 Translating Theory into Action for Autonomic Business

The book is intended for practitioners and executives interested in gaining a head start on understanding AI agents and identifying opportunities within their business to apply autonomic business concepts.

In the previous sections, we offered a historical perspective, examining technology waves and associated business model transformations up to AI agents and autonomic business (AB). This topic is further explored in Part I, 'Understanding the Autonomic Business', which delves into the details of AB, the underlying technologies, and real-world examples. Chap. 2, 'Maturity Levels and Evolution Path', focuses on measuring and scaling an autonomic business, laying out the entire spectrum of approaches to automating tasks, processes, decisions, and business goals from limited IT support in each of these areas to full autonomy. We also examine the limits of this approach and how the impacts on productivity may provide the business case for scaling AI technologies further to achieve higher levels of autonomy in systems.

Chapter 3, 'Technology Foundation of Autonomic Business', takes a deep dive into the underpinning technologies and how they are fused together to drive the AB

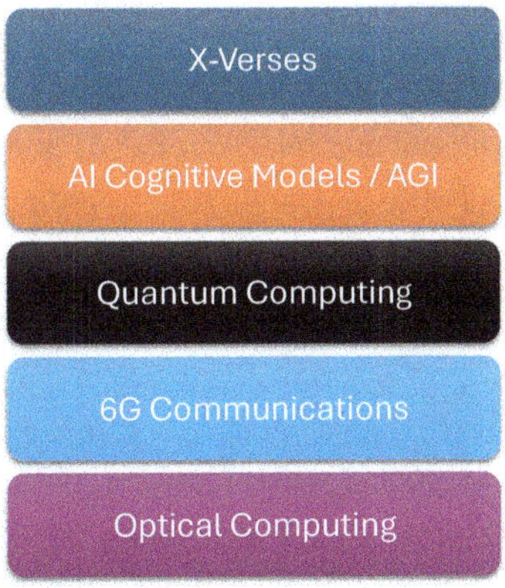

Fig. 1.3 A potential technology stack of the future

wave, primarily by AI but also by combining other emerging technologies. We explore how all these technologies are packaged together in AI agents and the key functional blocks of an advanced AI agent architecture. The chapter is kept at a high level so it is not a barrier for non-technical audiences to understand.

Chapter 4, 'Developing Multi-Agent Systems for Autonomic Business', adopts a more technical viewpoint explaining the key concepts behind architecting multi-agent systems including the design and functionalities of individual AI agents. A list of available Agent toolkits and frameworks is presented.

After explaining the technology, we explore examples of autonomic business in Chap. 5, 'Autonomic Business in the Real World'. A diverse range of real-world cases is explored, from AI agents performing customer service tasks to robotic agents in EV factories to autonomous operations and business models in retail stores, railways, telecommunication networks, and financial services. This chapter helps paint a picture of what is coming, showcasing several businesses already deploying semi-autonomous or fully autonomous technologies.

Part II, 'Autonomic Business Transformation', explores the ways in which we propose to manage AB, reflecting both the long-term view of what is needed and the more immediate requirements. Chapter 6, 'Evolving the Team', explores the organizational implications of AB across different phases of maturity, describes how to reshape the executive team to respond to the new challenges, and offers a template for creating an AB transformation blueprint. Chapter 7, 'New Capabilities and Challenges', elaborates further on the enterprise technical and operational capabilities required to underpin AB and highlights the potential challenges in their development, providing guidelines on how to mitigate them. Chapter 8, 'Developing an Autonomic Strategy and Business Architecture', is central to preparing for the long term by establishing a strategy for AB, developing an architecture centred on AI agents, and setting the proper foundation for governing agent operations at scale through establishing an Autonomic Business Operating System (ABOS).

Essential to the success of AI agents and, as a result, autonomic business is trusting the underlying technologies and systems. To achieve this, the necessary levels of oversight and control need to be established, including adhering to existing and upcoming regulatory requirements. This is detailed in Chap. 9, 'Instituting Control and Oversight', where we consider how to build trust within the organization towards AI technologies, look at the risks associated with the deployment of AI agents, and approaches to institute oversight and control, and examine the wider national and international AI governance and regulatory efforts.

Part III, 'The Future of Autonomic Business', focuses on the future opportunities from AI agents. Chapter 10, 'Agentic Ecosystems', is exploring how AB ecosystems may evolve to create a wider opportunity for AI-driven marketplaces where businesses and individuals trade services and products through AI agents. This concept of agentic ecosystems is clearly articulated, and emerging examples are presented in the context of travel and HR vertical sectors. Chapter 11, 'Robotics Revolution', takes the idea of AI agents one step further to its ultimate destination, which is that of intelligent robots becoming a reality, roaming the physical world and entering practical use across multiple enterprise sectors. The current landscape of robotic systems is explored along with examining the huge future potential in industrial and domestic applications.

The last chapter in the book is the 'Epilogue'. In this chapter, we summarize some of the findings and themes discussed throughout the book and position AI agents and AB in the context of a human-centric vision of the enterprise and the wider world. We focus on the opportunities from AB rather than the risks and how it can be approached as a positive force for change and enhancing human lives.

Part I
Understanding the Autonomic Business

Chapter 2
Maturity Levels and Evolution Path

As discussed in the introduction, autonomic business can encompass a range of outcomes, from simple forms of task or process automation supported by IT to autonomous AI agents orchestrating and executing tasks. Given the scale and diversity of organizations, there is bound to be an uneven application of AI and agentic

C. Voudouris, *Autonomic Business Transformation*, Management for Professionals, https://doi.org/10.1007/978-3-032-01415-3_2

technologies within an organization, making it challenging to measure and understand the level of maturity regarding the application of AI as a whole.

Without the ability to measure, it is difficult to understand how to improve and scale autonomic approaches and the application of AI agents within a business. At a high level, this can be seen as a journey from manual processes to automated processes, but this is likely just one dimension of an autonomic transformation journey. This journey is not new; several IT systems such as Enterprise Resource Planning (ERP), Customer Relationship Management (CRM), and Supply Chain Management (SCM) have, in one way or another, encoded these processes and workflows in their functionality, enabling best practices to become repetitive and adopted across entire verticals and industries.

We should be able to track several other dimensions beyond processes and their management. In a previous incarnation of the idea of digital workers, a set of technologies developed around robotic process automation (RPA) focused on automating not the management of processes but the underlying execution of tasks by machines [16]. Although the technology was brittle and not robust to changes, task execution is another useful dimension to measure the degree to which machines can replace humans in executing individual tasks within a workflow or process.

Thus far, one might claim there is no notion of autonomy or adaptivity, although a certain degree of agency may be exhibited by such systems. Adding decision-making automation at least provides robust agency characteristics and can certainly allow for adaptivity if there are learning aspects on how decisions are made and improved over time to optimize system performance. Thus, decision-making is another important dimension, especially if it encapsulates aspects of machine learning in the process. But isn't this what data and analytics (D&A) platforms and machine learning (ML) tools have been promising today, on top of BPM and RPA foundations?

What distinguishes AI agents that brings a new dimension previously unexplored by past automation innovations? The answer lies in the word 'autonomy' itself. What really distinguishes this wave compared to previous ones is the ability to give goals to systems and allow them to reason and coordinate to achieve them with limited or no human input. While this does not yet represent full autonomy, since humans still primarily define the overarching goals, it is easy to envision a future where human-driven goal setting occurs at increasingly strategic levels within the organization. In such a structure, AI agents operating at lower levels could autonomously establish their own sub-goals, effectively enabling a self-managing enterprise aligned with the broader objectives.

In summary, we can list these four dimensions where the Triple-A (Agency, Adaptivity, Autonomy) properties of AI agents can be leveraged within an autonomic business context:

Process automation.
Task execution.
Decision-making.
Goal setting.

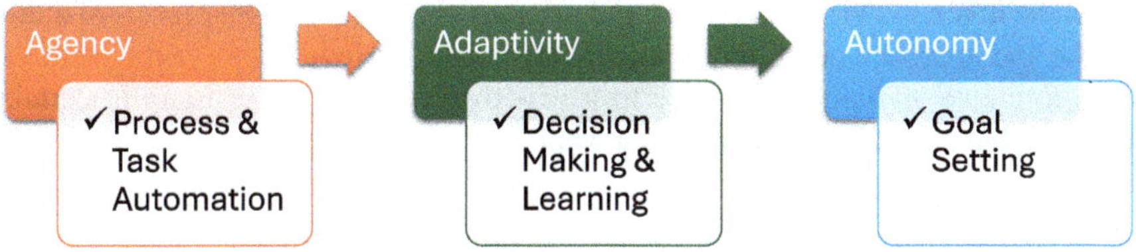

Fig. 2.1 Key business dimensions enabled by AI agent: Agency, Adaptivity, and Autonomy

The degree to which the above are still human-driven or machine-driven largely dictates the degree of autonomic behaviours exhibited within a business. Figure 2.1 depicts how process/task automation, decision-making, goal setting align with the Agency, Adaptivity, Autonomy as the key defining properties of AI agents.

2.1 Machine and Human Symbiosis

Across the four dimensions mentioned, the balance between human and machine input can vary widely. On one end, processes can be human-driven with minimal technological support, while on the other end, a machine-driven environment may require little human input, with humans primarily handling exceptions or approving AI actions.

To explain this spectrum of states, we define four levels as follows:

Human-driven: The majority of interactions are driven by humans with limited machine support.

Machine-assisted: The majority of interactions are driven by humans, but with tools aiding the effort.

Machine-collaborative: Machines play an increased role in performing tasks and share the load with human actors.

Machine-driven: The majority of interactions are driven by machines, with humans assuming supervisory roles and/or handling exceptions.

These states can apply separately to each dimension, such as process management, task execution, decision-making, and goal setting. The capabilities of AI dictate the extent to which human actors are displaced in each dimension, creating an order from easier to harder, where intelligence can play a bigger role:

Process management/workflows.
Individual task execution.
Decision-making.
Goal Setting.

Given the diversity within a business, some areas may exhibit higher levels of automation and approach autonomy, while others may not. How can we combine these ideas to create an autonomic scale to assess the prevailing behaviours in certain parts of a business or the business as a whole? We address that in the next section.

2.2 Defining an Autonomic Scale

It is often the case that someone reinvents the wheel when defining a new scale for a new domain. To avoid that here, we are not introducing a new scale; instead, we are adapting the existing SAE J3016 standard levels for autonomous vehicles [59, 60] and applying them to a business context.

This approach ensures that certain audiences will already be familiar with the concept. The SAE levels are also being adopted in other domains, such as Rail Automated Train Operation standards [61]. Therefore, it makes sense to map autonomic business (AB) to a recognized autonomy scale and model that is gaining traction in various fields, rather than creating a new framework from scratch.

Similar to the standards developed in the automotive industry for self-driving vehicles [59], an autonomic business exhibits different prevailing levels of automation, ranging from limited IT support to a fully autonomous business (→ Fig. 2.2):

Level 0 - Limited IT Support.
Level 1 - Human Assistance.
Level 2 - Human Augmentation.
Level 3 - Conditional Autonomy.
Level 4 - High Autonomy.
Level 5 - Full Autonomy.

In levels 1, 2, and 3, the business is primarily human-driven, with goal setting, decision-making, task execution, and process management partly or fully dependent on humans utilizing IT tools to varying degrees to realize the organization's business and operating models.

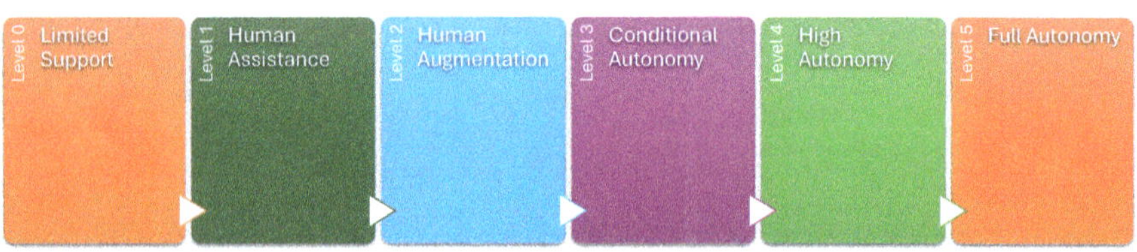

Fig. 2.2 The autonomic business scale

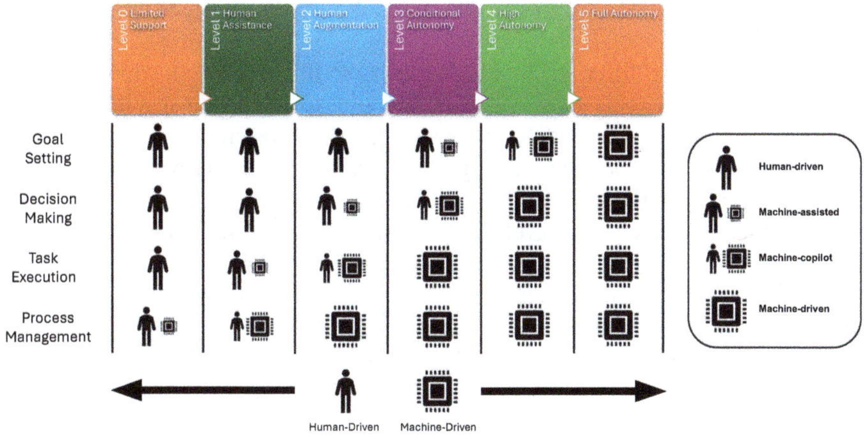

Fig. 2.3 Detailed view of the autonomic business scale across key business dimensions

In levels 4 and 5, the business is mainly machine-driven, with goal setting, decision-making, task execution, and process management partly or fully dependent on AI agents interacting with humans and other AI agents to realize the organization's business and operating models. Figure 2.3 depicts a more detailed view of the autonomic scale.

Mapping a business or parts of it across this framework, or creating a heatmap of key business functions, can be a valuable tool for understanding the maturity of a business. It can also help identify ways to move between levels, aiding in the strategizing and planning of an autonomic transformation journey.

It is reasonable to assume that most businesses are currently at levels 0–2, with a few exceptions reaching Level 3/4. We will explore examples of businesses in these higher levels in Chap. 5 later in the book.

2.3 Advancing Maturity Levels Through Enabling Technologies

Given the proliferation of IT in business since the mid-1980s, one can safely assume that Level 0, where limited support is in place to underpin process management through ERP, CRM, or SCM systems, is present in the majority of businesses today and has been for some time.

Moving to Level 1, where machines assist humans with task execution and drive most processes, can also be considered already in place, at least in medium to large enterprises. These organizations deploy tools to improve employee productivity, with CRM or ERP systems driving business workflows, although substantial human input is still required to handle exceptions and direct workflows. The use of RPA has also been partly successful over the past 2–3 years, increasing enterprise capabilities.

The situation may differ for Small Medium Enterprises (SMEs), which, beyond using common office tools, may lack dedicated tools to aid in their specific domains or enterprise systems to execute business workflows. However, the use of Software-as-a-S (SaaS) products has significantly improved the availability of software capabilities, especially in the last decade.

A key transition occurs at Level 2, which we call Human Augmentation. This is the leap many enterprises today attempt to make, utilizing previous generations of AI-supported technologies (e.g. data and analytics) and introducing new generative AI use cases and tools. Provided this builds on solid levels of process management and task automation, it has the potential for enterprises to reach best practice levels for their industry vertical without necessarily becoming early adopters of immature technologies and applications.

Despite the extensive use of technology at Level 2, the enterprise is still human-driven in its entirety, with systems lacking autonomic characteristics. However, agency and adaptivity can be exhibited depending on the degrees of automated decision-making and the provided process management and task execution automation.

This brings us to the next level of maturity, Level 3, which we call Conditional Autonomy. At this level, large parts of the work, including aspects of decision-making, are largely automated, with machines assisting in goal setting. However, humans are still responsible for setting these goals and acting in an override or corrective mode if exceptions occur.

Although few companies may fully operate at this level, individual units within organizations can exhibit Level 3 characteristics. For example, advanced planning and scheduling systems used in logistics or manufacturing operations represent a Level 3 type of organization, especially when considering the increased use of robotics in manufacturing or warehouse environments. We will examine such an example with the automotive factory of the future later in the book (see Sect. 5.2). Similarly, metro rail operations or certain automated transport systems can also be seen as exhibiting largely autonomous systems controlling the trains, with human override ensuring safety and compliance (see Sect. 5.3).

In a service context, we explored the concept of intelligent Service Chain Management in a previous book [62], focusing on the application of AI in automating the planning and scheduling of resources for service organizations, striving to achieve automation levels similar to those found in manufacturing environments through Supply Chain Management applications.

Recent cases of automation using generative AI agents for customer service, which we will also look at later in this book (see Sect. 5.1), exhibit similar scenarios to those found in manufacturing and transport, with a large part of customer interactions handled by AI agents.

One may appreciate that when the adoption of AI agents reaches across large parts of the organization, with multi-agent systems taking responsibility for running processes and executing tasks, we start reaching Level 4 of autonomy. We identified some cases, representing early examples of such scenarios, such as the operations of autonomous retail stores, management of telecom networks, and algorithmic trading in a fintech context.

Finally, we may consider Level 5, where AI agents are also involved in goal setting for large parts of an organization, exhibiting full autonomy. Such organizations do not currently exist, but one can imagine the potential at a small scale where AI runs a website or provides services within a very limited scope. Certainly, ideas on this have been suggested, though they are only experimental, and it will take some time to reach the mainstream. For medium and large organizations, that future is perhaps a decade away or even more. The enabling technologies mapped against the levels of autonomy are summarized in Fig. 2.4.

2.4 Human–Machine Interaction Across Maturity Levels

In traditional packaged application products that dominated the IT-enabled business era, business users accessed standardized application functionality through monolithic systems with little adaptability or configurability. As we moved into the digital era, applications became more modular and configurable. This resulted in the user interface (UI)/user experience (UX) becoming less tightly connected to the business logic layer, relying instead on APIs to access business logic functionality. Functionality also started to be delivered as composable components rather than monolithic application suites.

Despite an increased focus on user experience in the digital era and the ability to provide adaptive applications by decoupling business logic from the UI layer, there

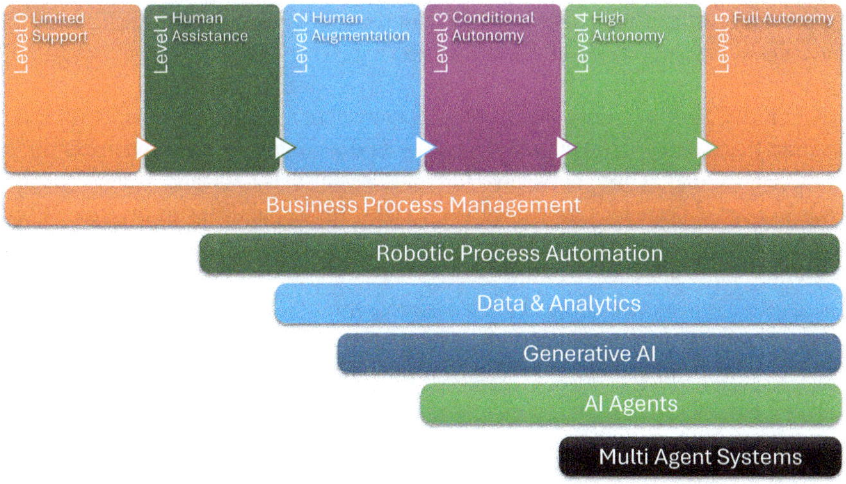

Fig. 2.4 Enabling technologies for different levels of the autonomic business scale

was little conceptual change in how humans interacted with tools for conducting their work. In some ways, this resulted in the massive productivity savings, often touted by large IT programs, failing to materialize.

Ultimately, the next evolution that will enable autonomic business will likely involve redefining the UI/UX to move towards an agentic user experience, where AI takes on the role of co-pilot or co-worker. Large language model (LLM) technologies will enable increasingly natural language interactions, initially in text format, with multimodal interactions between humans and anthropomorphic agents (also known as digital humans [63]) additionally envisaged whether these are replicas of real humans or synthetic personalities.

Agentic UX is a nascent topic, making it difficult to predict how it will develop. However, all the work done during the digital era to develop APIs and convert monolithic applications into configurable components can support this upcoming era. AI agents, through their agency characteristics, will be able to decide what tools or APIs to use to execute their actions. They will increasingly be able to compose new applications by assembling existing software components, requesting other agents to produce capabilities for them, or even authoring code as required to enact their processes and achieve their goals.

Goal setting and task delegation from humans to agents can be seen as a key new form of human–machine interaction, as seen now through prompting generative AI models and steering them towards desired effects. Similarly, the reverse may be experienced, with AI delegating tasks to human workers, as has recently been the case with *PaymanAI* [64].

As multi-agent systems take hold, the human role is moving towards the edge of platforms, with conversational agents interfacing with human process stakeholders and internal processes and tasks largely orchestrated and executed through agent-to-agent communications. Localized or centralized monitoring of agent operations may still involve human control and the ability to override decisions and actions in a supervisory role. This is no different from today's robotic factories, although the new context will largely be in the area of services where human involvement is still dominant.

Agentic UX is not only about human-to-machine interactions but also about machine-to-machine interactions, especially in the context of cross-business transactions. This distinction between Human-2-Agent (H-2-A) and Agent-2-Agent (A-2-A) user experiences may eventually cause the capabilities to diverge. While H-2-A has a limiting factor at present, A-2-A can be optimized and evolve into new forms or languages of communication. Historically, Agent Communication Language [38] is one example of such Agent Communication Protocol. Most recent developments in this area are the development of Model Context Protocol by Anthropic [49] and also the Agent2Agent protocol developed by Google [50] both of which will be explored later in this book. Even non-symbolic ways of exchanging information such as neural weights cannot be excluded (e.g. for the purposes of transfer learning between agents) or collaborative problem-solving. One such experiment is described in [65].

Although this has been the domain of sci-fi, human-to-agent neural interfaces can be envisaged in the twenty-to-thirty-year horizon, as explored by companies such as *Neuralink* [66].

This evolution from digital UX to agentic UX and the split between H-2-A and A-2-A, aligned with the requirements of the autonomic scale, is depicted in Fig. 2.5.

The H-2-A UI/UX is expected to receive intense focus over the next 2 years. Given the ability of agents to execute various tasks on behalf of the user, the notion of a largely static interface becomes insufficient to engage users across a variety of situations and information presentation needs that may arise during task execution. The ability to dynamically generate user interfaces based on task context becomes paramount. This 'Generative UI' is already the target and ambition of a startup called *'/dev/agents'*, created by former Android leaders aiming to build the equivalent of an operating system for AI agents [67].

A similar concept based on generative principles is the creation of avatars on demand, customized for different industries and situations. These digital humans can even take the form and mimic their users after a short period of training [68]. In a way, human users cannot be in different places at the same time, but their avatars can do that so they effectively represent them. Similarly, businesses can train digital humans to facilitate H-2-A interactions with their clients. These digital humans can serve many customers simultaneously, which is a current limitation with single human operators. Training these models on specific domain data can prevent AI agents from responding to arbitrary requests outside the business's domain.

NVIDIA unveiled such a prototype AI avatar at Computer Electronics Show (CES) 2025 called R2X [69]. The R2X is rendered and animated using NVIDIA's

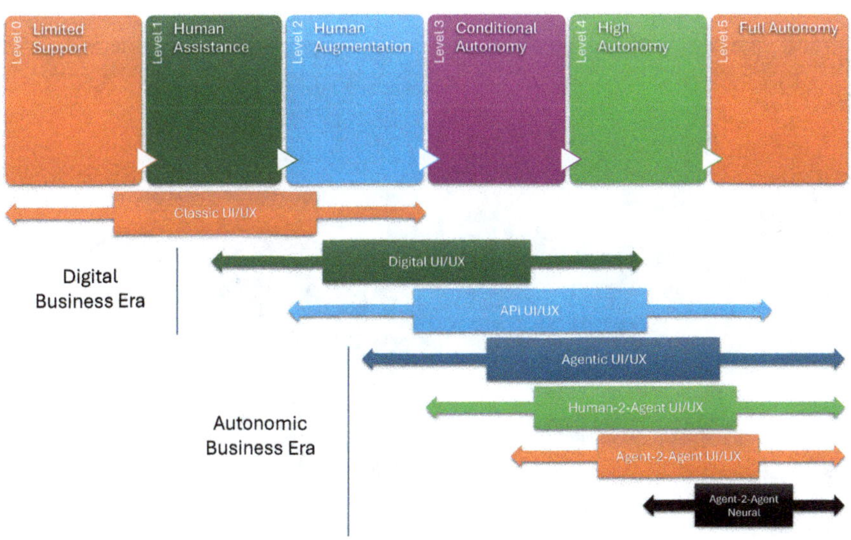

Fig. 2.5 Evolution of UI/UX across the autonomic business scale and the emergence of agentic UI/UX

AI models, and users can run the avatar on popular LLMs of their choice, such as OpenAI's GPT-4o [70] or xAI's Grok [71]. Users can interact with R2X through text and voice, upload files for processing, or allow the AI assistant to view what's happening on their screen or through their camera (→ Fig. 2.6).

2.5 Autonomic Business Timing and Impact

As with many strategic technology trends, the impact profile may be spread over several years. The typical adoption of new technologies is characterized by the S-curve model, while the hype cycle introduced by Gartner captures the expectation side of technology. In their 2024 Hype Cycle for Generative AI [72], Gartner considers autonomous agents as having a transformational impact over the next 10 years. However, views differ on this, with tech sector executives like Eric Schmidt predicting such impacts may occur sooner, within the next 2–3 years [73].

Relying on historical precedent, technology adoption curves are compressed and accelerated over time. This was demonstrated by Michael Felton in his *New York Times* article, which showed adoption curves for computers, cell phones, and the Internet spreading within decades or less [74]. These curves were compared to more fundamental innovations such as the telephone, automobile, and electricity, which took several decades to reach similar levels (→ Fig. 2.7).

Therefore, it is not unreasonable to expect that AI, and more specifically innovations founded on agentic AI such as autonomic business, will develop faster than previous waves.

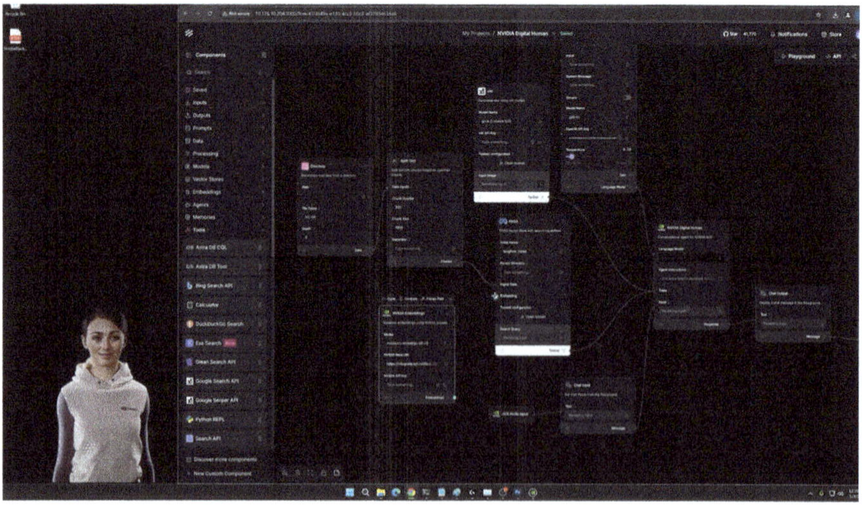

Fig. 2.6 Example of humanoid avatar created by NVIDIA interacting with the user. *Source*: NVIDIA

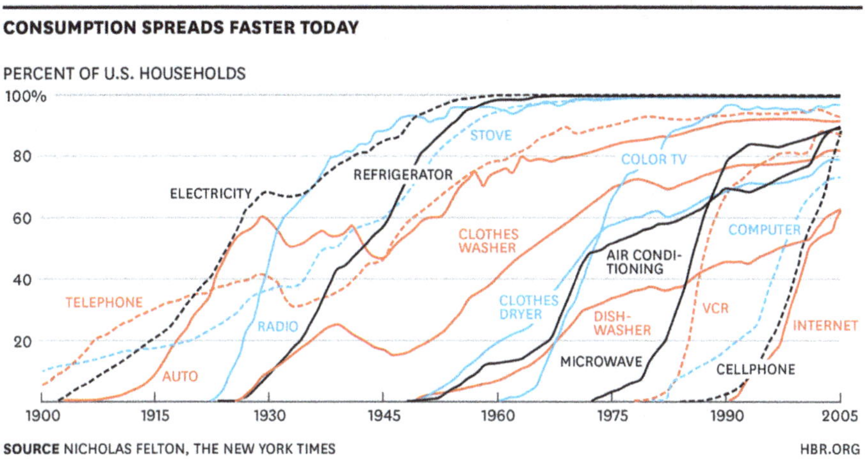

Fig. 2.7 Technology adoption is accelerating over the decades

Several factors support this hypothesis. Investment in AI agents is accelerating, as indicated by recent reports (e.g. by CB Insights [25]). Major technology giants such as Microsoft, Meta, Google, Amazon, Nvidia, Salesforce, and others are not only increasing their investments in AI but are also focusing more on AI agents in their recent announcements [75–80]. Additionally, a plethora of smaller players and startups are working from the bottom-up, trying to disrupt the main players and gain a foothold in other horizontal agentic platforms or vertical applications. The scaling hypothesis suggests that frontier models will grow by several factors of x10 in capabilities, potentially reaching near-AGI capabilities sooner rather than later. Furthermore, combining innovations from AI and other technologies can have a combinatorial innovation effect, accelerating this present wave more than previous ones.

However, none of the above is a foregone conclusion. There are doubts about whether the reasoning capabilities of agents can be trusted as robust and reliable [81]. This touches on the core argument of whether neural networks can reason similarly to symbolic approaches to logic or be even better at processing language than anything ever produced by classical Linguistics as argued by Geoffrey Hinton [82]. The knowledge available on the Internet is limited and even referred to as the 'fossil fuel' of AI [83], so LLMs may face barriers in finding additional information to train on. The scalability of agent ecosystems may also come into question too, given the complexity of these systems and the potential lack of effective coordination mechanisms when they reach a certain scale. Additionally, there is the threat of governments imposing restrictions due to perceived or real cybersecurity or safety risks, especially concerning physical AI systems.

2.6 Model Scaling and Productivity Savings

Neural networks are not a new approach to AI, but their recent success is largely due to the scaling effect, where more data and larger neural networks produce far superior results. This progress was made possible by the advent of the Internet and the wider availability of large datasets. Looking back, the success of the ImageNet project in 2013 in vision and object recognition was a starting point [84], demonstrating the power of deep learning powered by GPUs, yielding impressive results. Another milestone was the AlphaGo algorithm [85], which decisively defeated one of the world's best players using Google's reinforcement learning algorithm.

The first transformer paper, which is the technology behind today's large language models (LLMs), was published in 2017 [86]. OpenAI used this technology in GPT-1 [87] and GPT-2 [88], released in 2018 and 2019, respectively. GPT-2 demonstrated the scaling concept, where a tenfold increase in parameter count and training set size significantly improved its capabilities compared to GPT-1. This was somewhat expected, given that previous approaches to natural language processing (NLP) relied on supervised learning and heavily annotated datasets. This caused a 'Eureka' moment, primarily due to scale, and as it was later described by Bill Gates, he thought this was 'the most important advance in technology since the graphical user interface' [89].

This has resulted in ever-increasing efforts to train even larger models with orders of magnitude more parameters and network layers. Training these models to achieve the next level of performance can easily cost hundreds of millions of dollars. Assuming we continue to see a 4x growth in scaling over the coming years, it may require several billion dollars to make the next jump purely through scaling. There are, of course, algorithmic improvements using reasoning approaches to call an LLM multiple times to solve challenging benchmarks and AGI tests, giving credit to the claim that we are perhaps an algorithm away from AGI, even using some of today's so-called frontier models.

However, there are limits to this scaling in terms of improving performance as the model scales, assuming the multi-billion price tag can be afforded to create the so-called *AI gigafactories* [24] to make it happen. The rule is empirical, and there are practical issues as the models scale, which fall into four areas [90]:

Power constraints: As models grow, it takes several months to train and fine-tune them. This puts an enormous burden on power requirements, even by industrial standards, requiring several gigawatts to power AI operations.

Chip production: Graphic Processing Units (GPUs) and other alternatives such as AI Application-Specific Integrated Circuits (ASICs) are required in large quantities to develop a frontier model. For example, xAI's development of the Grok 2.3 large language model required a supercluster called Colossus, comprising 100,000 GPUs [91]. There is limited supply capacity from hardware manufacturers, making it difficult, not to mention potential supply chain disruptions due to geopolitical tensions or regional wars.

Data scarcity: Data used for training general frontier models primarily includes all Internet data, but that is finite. Unless synthetic data can be produced, it will become increasingly hard to find new data to improve model scaling. This is why data has been called the 'fossil fuel' of AI, given that it is a finite resource [83]. Obviously, multimodal or enterprise data can be utilized, but that will be finite too. Moreover, the cost of accessing data is increasing as providers such as Reddit, NY Times and others either gate their data from AI crawlers or start charging for API access. Unless synthetic data closes the gap, large models will not be able to train on datasets of the required size to make use of the additional dimensions in the neural network [92]. Symbolic AI may help by inferring new knowledge creating 'reasoning' feedback loops enriching and augmenting existing datasets.

Latency wall: As models get bigger, more sequential operations are required to train them. This leads to speed limits due to the latency of modern GPU setups [90].

It is also important not to underestimate the scale of the learning models themselves, which leads to issues and errors when coding and training over long periods, introducing implementation risks found in similar complex and convoluted engineering projects.

Assuming most of the above barriers can be overcome, the multi-billion price tag of developing even larger and more advanced frontier models needs to have a realistic business justification. There is an irrevocable link between autonomic business and generative AI. Autonomic business needs to justify generative AI investments, and generative AI investments are needed to make autonomic business happen. To understand the scale of potential cost savings, consider that global labour compensation is approximately $60 trillion per year [93]. Even without factoring in accelerated economic growth from AI automation, if it becomes feasible to develop AI capable of effectively substituting human labour, investing billions in AI gigafactories or projects of that scale to capture even a fraction of this $60 trillion flow would be economically justified.

Given this potential, achieving complete or near-complete automation earlier could be worth a substantial portion of global output, let alone a few billion dollars. Recognizing this immense value, investors may redirect significant portions of their capital from traditional sectors into AI development and its essential infrastructure (energy production and distribution, semiconductor fabrication plants, data centres). This potential for unprecedented economic growth could drive trillions of dollars in investment in AI development [90].

However, there is an opposing viewpoint on productivity benefits. Daron Acemoglu, Institute Professor at MIT, estimates that only a quarter of AI-exposed tasks will be cost-effective to automate within the next 10 years, implying that AI will impact less than 5% of all tasks. He forecasts that AI will increase US productivity by only 0.5% and GDP growth by only 0.9% cumulatively over the next decade [94]. He also questions whether AI adoption will create new tasks and products, saying these impacts are 'not a law of nature'.

Ultimately, it is too early to predict with certainty how this will play out. Will AI impact global productivity by a large percentage or have a very small impact, even for advanced economies? It is the use of AI to realize autonomic business that will have to prove the point, as AI agents using sophisticated LLMs or other cognitive models seamlessly integrate into existing workflows, manipulate browser windows or virtual machines, and operate independently in the background. These agents will eventually look and feel like 'employees'. As with many other technologies over the years, it will take a little longer for that to happen and for human trust to be established. Even if that happens, it will be the job of humans for a while to manage them, ensure they're safe, and oversee their security.

2.7 Disrupting the Disruptors

The development of new large language models has become an expensive endeavour, akin to the economics of heavy industries like steel. At the end of the day, new AI gigafactories will require 'giga-investments' and better have a 'giga-payback'. Constrained funding flows may result in larger models being released at slower rates, with improvements becoming more marginal and primarily focused on the 'long tail' of knowledge. This area, where correlations can be made across disciplines and domains, has traditionally been challenging for humans, who tend to specialize in specific fields. Making connections across disciplines may lead to dramatic innovations in areas such as biology which could be transformative for certain industries (e.g. pharmaceuticals) but, as well, it may prove a highly risky endeavour should these breakthroughs fail to materialize.

Open-sourcing large language models will also become increasingly questionable for investors in these organizations. Even if these models are open-sourced, significant costs will remain in inference rather than training for those that want to use them. The industry, which positions itself as a disruptor, can be disrupted by advancements in algorithms that achieve similar performance to scaled-up large language models at a fraction of the cost. This can be accomplished through different training methods, as demonstrated by the Chinese startup DeepSeek [95], or through improved reasoning at inference time, where a model is invoked multiple times to refine its responses. These approaches can produce results that would typically require a significantly scaled-up model, as shown by OpenAI's o1, o3, and o4-mini models [96].

There is a substantial risk of spending hundreds of billions on assembling a complex hardware platform, requiring massive amounts of energy, and scrambling to find new sources of data or generate more using synthetic data, only to be outpaced by an unknown startup that innovates on top of a smaller and cheaper to use open-source model. We believe the balance will shift from mounting huge efforts to continue scaling models to becoming more efficient algorithmically at both training and inference time to achieve similar levels of improvement.

Chapter 3
Technology Foundations of Autonomic Business

Autonomic business heavily relies on combining technological advancements that, individually, are not sufficient to enable it. It is the combination of these technologies, collectively referred to as agentic AI, that has provided the foundation for

C. Voudouris, *Autonomic Business Transformation*, Management for Professionals, https://doi.org/10.1007/978-3-032-01415-3_3

building AI agents and the emergence of autonomic business as a result. It has been a long journey for some of these technologies.

In this chapter, we explore the core technologies and innovations behind agentic AI, enabling technologies that can amplify the impact of AI agents in both the digital and physical worlds and finally explore some promising directions that may have a profound impact on the area over the coming years.

3.1 The Rise of AI Agents

Agentic AI is not entirely new, but the term emerged more prominently in the second half of 2024 to describe the next level of AI advancements following generative AI.

The concept of agent-based computing has its roots in the 1990s and 2000s [7]. It extends component-based approaches that dominated software and application thinking from the days of object-oriented programming to cloud-native container-based applications. AI agents offer a way to design complex systems by modelling them as a set of multiple distinct and independent functional components. Furthermore, AI agents enable the aggregation of different functionalities such as planning, reasoning, learning, and coordination into a cohesive whole.

The first AI agent standards were developed by FIPA in the late 1990s and early 2000s, aiming to define how to implement agent platforms and how these platforms should interoperate [31]. Despite several agent platforms adopting the FIPA standards, such as JADE [39], Zeus [40], and FIPA OS [98], this initial attempt at AI agents did not gain commercial momentum or practical use cases beyond the early examples.

While the area of AI agents became dormant from a commercial perspective in the mid-2000s, the rise of the Internet and mobile technologies realized an interconnected and mobile world, empowering individuals and societies while democratizing the distribution of content and information. This was followed by data and cloud technologies taking centre stage and reaching global scale, dramatically increasing processing power and storage. Digesting terabytes of web and other data, deep learning algorithms became capable of encoding patterns of human intelligence into compact neural network models, developing an implicit 'world model' to reason about. These algorithms and models, along with other technologies, are now combining to provide the foundations for autonomic business.

3.2 Core Agentic Technologies

As large language models (LLMs) have demonstrated impressive capabilities and gained immense popularity, researchers have begun leveraging these models to construct AI agents. A pivotal moment in enhancing the capabilities of these agents was the introduction of LLMs as the main planning and reasoning engine. This step did not happen overnight and is still ongoing.

Specifically, LLMs are employed as the primary component of the 'brain' or controller of these agents, expanding their perceptual and action space through strategies such as multimodal perception and tool utilization. These LLM-based agents can exhibit reasoning and planning abilities comparable to symbolic agents. They can also acquire interactive capabilities with the environment by learning from feedback and performing new actions. Additionally, LLMs undergo pre-training on large-scale corpora and demonstrate the capacity for generalization, allowing for seamless transfer between tasks without the need to update parameters, which underpins agent versatility.

While several foundational models are now widely available, they are still not sufficient to reason and plan as a complete functioning 'brain' for agents, moving away from the disappointing and often frustrating experience users had with the first generation of chatbots. However, given the intense R&D efforts in this area, significant improvements in capabilities are expected over the next 12–24 months.

Let us explore some of the key technological developments behind the emerging generation of LLM-powered AI agents.

3.2.1 Planning and Reasoning

With every new iteration of frontier models such as Claude (Anthropic) [99], Grok (xAI) [100], GPT (OpenAI) [101], Llama (Meta) [102], and Gemini (Google) [103], we can expect capabilities to continue improving proportionally to the scale of the model. This matters in a couple of ways for realizing this new generation of AI agents.

Firstly, while specific communication languages were previously defined for agents (such as ACL defined by FIPA [38]) to exchange messages between them, and human-to-agent interfaces were rather bespoke, this new generation of agents can utilize their LLM engine to communicate in natural language or using multimodal inputs. This greatly simplifies human-to-agent communication, making it universally applicable thus removing the need for specialized input methods.

Secondly, the planning and reasoning capabilities, previously based primarily on rules or other symbolic AI approaches, can now be approached using techniques such as Chain of Thought (CoT) [104] and ReAct [105], prompting the LLM to plan the steps required to reach a goal. This prompting can be done behind the scenes as part of the reasoning logic of the tool rather than requiring repeated human input.

One might question whether the capabilities of LLMs can replace the deep and precise planning exemplified by goal-driven workflows, rules, or other symbolic AI approaches. This is a valid concern. Fundamental to reasoning is the ability to have a model of the world to reason about how to achieve one's goals.

For symbolic agents to reason effectively, they were typically equipped with an ontology describing the domain they operated in and well-defined planning algorithms to search the space of possible solutions to achieve a certain goal. Techniques such as partial order planning [106] were used to schedule and execute actions. The question arises: is all of this still needed, or can the LLM model undertake these tasks?

The answer lies somewhere in between, at least for this generation of LLMs, which makes AI agents a powerful way to extend LLM capabilities. LLMs may be internally learning a model of the world that goes beyond statistical correlations between words, and there is research pointing to some evidence of this [107]. However, this internal model of the world developed by LLMs is not yet accurate and powerful enough to replace the deep and precise approach often required to solve real-world problems or execute enterprise processes.

Wrapping an LLM inside an agent and addressing its deficiencies by providing more structured and programmatic logic, such as workflows, explicit standard operating procedures, structured roles, and communication protocols in a multi-agent context (e.g. MCP [49] and Agent2Agent [50]), can overcome these limitations until the next generation of models improves and becomes more capable of navigating an enterprise as a human employee can do today.

According to the Berkeley Artificial Intelligence Research (BAIR) team [108], composite systems are easier to improve, are more dynamic than single LLMs, and have more flexibility in terms of meeting user-specific performance (and cost) goals. They are also arguably more controllable and trustworthy, as composite outputs can be filtered and vetted by other components instead of relying on a single source of truth (a lone LLM).

3.2.2 *Use of APIs and Tools*

Among the various capabilities that LLMs can be trained on are writing API calls and utilizing third-party tools. Techniques such as Gorilla [109], Toolformer [110], and APIgen [111] can enhance the LLM's ability to utilize millions of APIs and tools, rather than just refining its conversational skills.

Commonly incorporated tools include web browsing, calculators, translation systems, and Python interpreters. API calls function similarly to tool usage, allowing the LLM to significantly expand its capabilities without dealing with low-level implementation details.

One limitation is the inability of certain LLMs to use tools in a chain (i.e. using the output of one tool as the input for another tool). This is because API calls for each tool are generated independently; consequently, there are no examples of chained tool use in the training datasets. Additionally, the LLM-based agent has often the API and tool logic hard-coded into its model, rather than being able to call other agents depending on the context and tap into additional tools and APIs. This last limitation has been addressed with protocols which allow for such external tool and API use as these are described in the next section.

3.2.3 Communication and Coordination

Beyond single AI agents, multi-agent systems involve several AI agents collaborating to achieve a user goal. Striking the right balance between autonomy and alignment emerges as a central challenge in LLM-powered multi-agent systems. These systems must navigate a fine line—being autonomous enough to manage the interplay between multiple LLM-powered agents while remaining aligned with user intentions and goals.

Most current LLM-based multi-agent frameworks utilize unconstrained natural language as a communication interface. Despite the versatility of natural language, a question arises: does pure natural language communication suffice for solving complex tasks? For example, in the telephone game (or Chinese whispers), after several rounds of communication, the original information may become distorted, so it is difficult to encode things like *standard operating procedures* [263].

Similar to the Agent Communication Language [38] developed under FIPA standards [31], a new wave of communication protocols is emerging for LLM-powered agents to enable multi-agent system development. The focus is on standardizing how AI agents can:

Access external tools, data, and information sources.

Communicate and coordinate with each other across platforms.

The Model Context Protocol (MCP) developed by Anthropic [49], which has received wide publicity and adoption, addresses the first need. It significantly enhances AI agents' capabilities by enabling direct, bi-directional communication with external systems. This advancement allows AI agents to access real-time information from external databases, manage file systems, and interact seamlessly with external platforms. Agent2Agent (A2A), developed by Google, focuses on the second need of cross-agent communication and coordination [50]. The Agent Communication Protocol (ACP) developed by IBM [112, 113], originally inspired by MCP, is evolving towards discovery, delegation, and multi-agent orchestration features. A recent addition, as of March 2025, is Cisco's AGNTCY, which offers capabilities in agent discovery, identity, messaging, and observability, while also integrating with A2A and MCP [270].

It is inevitable that further variations of structured communication protocols such as MCP, A2A, ACP and AGNTCY will emerge to facilitate and streamline the communication of agents and expand access to external resources and services [114].

Furthermore, internal agent definitions are also becoming more structured and formalized, for example, by establishing a schema and format for each agent role in a multi-agent system and requesting that individual agents provide the necessary outputs based on their specific role and context. This approach ensures that agents and contextual resources can accomplish complex tasks consisting of various interconnected sub-tasks while remaining adequately aligned with the intentions and goals of their users.

3.2.4 Ontologies and Digital Twins

An ontology is a semantic component widely used in multi-agent systems (MAS) that formally describes knowledge as a set of concepts within a domain and the relationships between them. Ontologies formalize the structure of knowledge by defining concepts and relationships within a specific domain, relying on an underlying database structure to store and retrieve information. Similarly, a digital twin (DT) is used to facilitate the storage of knowledge, acting as an extensive database that stores and provides real-time access to data [115].

The most common way of representing knowledge is through ontologies. Ontologies are used to manage the knowledge of the physical world in the cyber-world, powered by real data obtained by the DT. In such cases, ontologies are used as tools to digitize the knowledge of the environment and physical objects needed by the agents to make decisions. This use of ontologies improves and facilitates interaction between agents. Moreover, DTs are sometimes seen as databases. In these cases, the DTs of different physical entities represent large knowledge databases that agents can observe, make decisions based on, and act upon.

The concept of the digital twin of the organization (DTO) shares many similarities with the concept of digital twins but applies it to a whole organization and its processes [116, 117, 220]. In contrast to digital twins in manufacturing, where data for modelling are derived from IoT (Internet of Things) sensors, DTO data about the progress of organizational business processes are received from information systems.

By expanding the digital twin idea from digital representations of physical items to include digital representations of the entire organization, a DTO acts as a living digital simulation model of the organization that updates and develops as the company grows. It also allows scenarios to be fully evaluated to anticipate the performance of prospective tactics and plans once ready.

Ontologies and digital twins will play an ever-increasing role as AI agents get applied in enterprise context both to formalize the concepts and relationships within the specific business domain so that multi-agent systems can function on a shared common understanding of business definitions and to allow for simulation and what-if scenario modelling so AI agents can test different tactics or strategies before taking decisions that impact the real business.

3.2.5 Large Action and Multimodal Models

While LLMs are trained to understand words and phrases and create original, grammatically correct text, large action models (LAMs) are advanced AI models that understand language and can 'think' through tasks to get things done [118, 119]. They can handle different kinds of information such as pictures, videos, and sounds, making them work more like how humans use digital content. Benefits of LAMs include:

Cost reductions: By automating tasks, reducing errors, and using resources more efficiently.

Improved decision-making: LLMs offer information, and LAMs take actions based on that information, leading to faster and more data-driven decisions.

New business models: By combining understanding and action, companies can create completely new services, such as automatic customer service systems, self-running warehouses, or AI-powered product design.

LAMs are gaining traction as a sophisticated alternative to traditional robotic process automation. Companies like Automation Anywhere and UiPath have begun integrating generative AI into their existing RPA toolkits, yet a new startup, Orby AI, is challenging these established players [120]. Orby's LAM simply observes a user at work, learns what can be automated, and creates the actions to implement it. Users then approve the process and can modify the actions at any time; this allows continuous improvement as Orby learns more.

The key advantage of LAMs lies in their capacity for adaptive learning and context-aware decision-making. Unlike RPA, which typically relies on rule-based logic, LAMs can assess situations and generate appropriate responses in real time. This adaptability is invaluable in industries such as finance and healthcare, where conditions can rapidly fluctuate.

There is potential for large multimodal models (LMMs) to be the main engine for creating a LAM. LMMs can process and understand multiple types of data modalities. These multimodal data can include text, images, audio, video, and potentially others. ÉCLAIR described in [121] provides a good example and overview of the approach. Through the use of LMMs and learning directly from users, ÉCLAIR addresses three main shortcomings of traditional process mining and RPA (high setup costs, brittle execution, and burdensome maintenance). Approaches such as ECLAIR and Orby can help achieve the promise of enterprise workflow automation. This topic is explored further in the context of agent-based business process management below.

3.2.6 Process Management and Workflow Execution

Agent-based business process management has already been realized at the prototype level during past work of the author [33], where business logic was coded into service definitions executable by a workflow engine, with goals set by the agents achieved through invocations of these workflows. However, there were two drawbacks to the approach. First, it had shortcomings in dealing with uncertainty, especially as reflected in exceptions in processes, which caused process flows to halt and require human intervention. Secondly, the approach had difficulty integrating with existing systems through the use of APIs, which were not well developed at the time. LLM-based Agents utilizing frameworks such as MCP and Agent2Agent can overcome these issues opening new horizons to realize autonomic processes and business operations orchestrated and executed by AI agents. However, architecture and design questions come into the fore.

Creating a multi-agent workflow for a given process can involve many decisions, such as how many agents to include, how to assign agent roles and capabilities, how the agents should interact with each other, and whether to automate a particular part of the workflow. There may not be a one-size-fits-all answer, and the best solution might depend on the specific application. This raises important questions: For what types of tasks and applications are multi-agent workflows most useful? How do multiple agents help in different applications? For a given task, what is the optimal (e.g. cost-effective) multi-agent workflow?

We delve into this topic in Chap. 4 where we examine in more detail how to design a multi-agent system (MAS) to underpin an autonomic business.

3.3 Enabling Technologies

AI agents will have limited abilities to operate in either digital or physical worlds unless they are enabled by a host of other technologies that are not directly linked to AI but, nonetheless, they are essential to provide connectivity, access to data and software, ability to control the environment, traceability, and security. We list these key enabling technologies for AI agents below.

3.3.1 5G and Internet of Things

As AI agents start to operate in the physical world in the context of autonomous vehicles, drones, or even domestic robots, the need for wireless communications becomes important as well as the ability to connect to individual devices on the network to perform tasks or collect data. A couple of technologies in the form of 5G networks [122] and Internet of Things [123] can now enable a wireless interconnected world making the job easier for AI agents to be applied in domains not strictly confined to the virtual side but also increasingly in robotic applications which will gradually emerge as the capabilities of AI agents extend to navigating physical worlds and manipulating objects.

3.3.2 APIs, Components, and Cloud-Native Apps

As part of the digital era, a whole host of legacy systems have been either reengineered into components and moved onto the cloud (e.g. cloud-native development) or now exposing their functionality and data through a comprehensive set of APIs opening up their architecture. This is in sharp contrast to the monolithic ERP and CRM systems of the past.

An important element of modern AI agent systems is the ability to access these APIs and applications/components to perform various tasks as required to achieve their goals and objectives. The availability of so many tools and APIs as well as code in the form of open source is providing a rich environment for agents to perform complex tasks by assembling composite functionalities in real time through 'gluing' together tools, components, and API.

3.3.3 Immersive Experiences

Immersive experiences and in particular the concept of the Metaverse [55] had attracted significant attention prior to the advent of generative AI. For a period of the time in the early 2020s, it looked as if this was going to be the dominant technology trend. Despite the investment from digital giants such as Facebook and Apple, the area did not grow as significantly as predicted.

Nonetheless, the capabilities developed in the form of virtual worlds and blending of the physical and digital can be utilized by AI agents to communicate in the form of digital humans creating a mixed reality view where AI agents and humans through their avatars can coexist. It may be the case that it will be indistinguishable to interact with AI agents instead of humans in these virtual worlds and this comes with its own risks too [124].

Furthermore, digital representations of the physical world can also have other uses for AI agents allowing them to train using 'replicas' of the physical world ahead of real-world deployments with fields such as autonomous cars already benefiting from testing their technologies in such virtual simulation environments [125].

3.3.4 Smart Sensors and Actuators, Smart Environments

An area often ignored but also of significant importance in the advancement of AI agents and other domains is that of smart sensor technologies [126]. Modern environments from smart buildings to smart cities to smart cars are equipped with arrays of sensors and actuators which can capture multiple streams of data (video, sound, temperature, humidity, etc.) and adjust parameters in real data to meet human preferences. Proliferation of these sensors and actuators means that even a single modern vehicle may be instrumented with 100 s of devices all networked together and acting as one intelligent system.

Intelligent assistants can be layered onto smart cars, buildings, or even entire smart cities, autonomously working to optimize human environments in line with user goals and directives. Once again, it's not just AI agents alone, but a suite of complementary technologies that enable the instrumentation and dynamic adjustment of these smart environments.

3.3.5 *Blockchain*

There is an expectation that AI agents will handle the majority of blockchain transactions in the near future. This is due to the combination of blockchain's transparent ledger and smart contracts being an excellent infrastructure choice for AI agents, enabling them to operate their own wallets and verify data rights and provenance for the information they use to make decisions [268]. Data and intellectual property rights are becoming increasingly sensitive issues, with high-profile cases involving newspapers and songwriters objecting to their intellectual property being used to train AI systems.

Users can own and safely monetize their data using NFTs, while AI agents can securely use this data without infringing on IP rights, allowing them to learn and evolve. Blockchain can facilitate such win-win scenarios. In an agent-driven web economy, smart contracts will also play a central role, with AI agents, for example, arranging payments for goods and services only once delivery is confirmed or service level agreements have been met.

Additionally, blockchain's decentralized, immutable ledger system provides a secure and auditable way to record and share agent decisions in multi-agent systems. This ensures traceability and accountability for autonomous agents and their actions [127].

3.4 What's the Next Big Thing in Agentic Technologies?

Closing the previous chapter, we discussed how developments in algorithms can disrupt big investments in scaling large language models. In this section, we highlight three disruptive technologies which hold a lot of promise in the two-to-five-year time horizon in the context of the AI technological period and autonomic business era.

3.4.1 *Reinforcement Learning*

Reinforcement learning (RL) is a form of machine learning that enables AI agents to learn to take actions in dynamic environments to maximize a specific reward signal [128]. Using RL, an AI agent can learn to perform a task through trial and error, without any prior knowledge.

A core concept in RL is the exploration–exploitation trade-off. The AI agent must explore its environment and try new actions to discover which ones yield rewards (exploration) while also preferring actions that have previously been rewarded (exploitation). The agent must balance these two approaches, continuously trying new actions while favouring those likely to lead to higher rewards.

In an enterprise context, an AI agent can be set a goal to achieve a specific outcome. If a reward signal can be defined for actions that bring the agent closer to this outcome, RL can be applied to guide the agent without the need for prior learning or training.

Although this example is simple and generic, it demonstrates the power and potential of RL to be applied in dynamic and unpredictable environments, such as enterprises. It can enable agents to achieve specific objectives without the overhead of extensive and costly training phases.

3.4.2 Combining Neural and Symbolic AI

Symbolic AI and Neural AI do not necessarily compete for application to the same problem; instead, they can be combined [131], with each approach playing to its strengths. Neural networks, through deep learning, can recognize patterns in images, such as the placement of objects in the real world. Consequently, Convolutional Neural Networks (CNNs) [129] and Recurrent Neural Networks (RNNs) [130] have become popular for tasks like image and speech recognition.

Meanwhile, symbolic AI and modelling approaches, such as knowledge graphs, can formally model the information held by CNNs or RNNs into a framework for validation, explanation, and reasoning. Combining symbolic and neural approaches enables AI agents to enhance their logic and reasoning capabilities, increasing their ability to explain how they arrived at certain decisions and making it easier to validate these decisions.

Symbolic AI may also accelerate training and inference on the neural side, improving the economics of AI, which are currently questionable, especially when creating ever-larger models that cost hundreds of billions each. If certain knowledge can be codified using symbolic approaches, this can act as a 'data compression' technique to reduce the overall size of neural networks required to achieve specific performance levels.

Last but not least, symbolic AI through its inferencing capabilities can enrich and augment existing knowledge and information giving rise to the intelligent ways of generating synthetic data for training LLMs.

3.4.3 Technology Fusion for Physical AI Agents

The fusion of technologies is crucial for enabling physically embodied AI, allowing autonomous agents to operate effectively in the real world. Consider the example of an autonomous car. Several advanced sensors, such as cameras, LIDAR, ultrasound, and radar, are required to provide the car with an accurate model of its surroundings. This data needs to be processed by AI techniques, such as neural networks, to understand the vehicle's environment and accurately assess the situation. Specialized GPU hardware for neural inference may be installed on board to meet the real-time requirements of the automotive domain.

LLM-based technologies may be used to manage interactions with vehicle users, executing their commands through a natural language interface. More deterministic, rule-based processing may be applied to control steering, acceleration, and braking. Advanced modelling may be needed to accurately predict the future movements of other cars or pedestrians, with some approaches utilizing agent-based modelling and simulation.

Furthermore, an autonomous vehicle may rely on 5G/6G communications to exchange information with cloud servers, for example, to plan routes to reach the desired destination. Realizing a complex physical autonomous system requires the fusion and combination of multiple technologies to create such an innovative system and application.

Similarly to autonomous vehicles, domestic robots based on LLM-based agents can be developed through tech fusion becoming something for everyone to own to improve their daily lives like the next car or major home appliance. The same applies to autonomic businesses and incorporating a large robotic workforce to automate large parts of manual work. This 'robotics' phase of AI agents through fusing with other technologies may be in itself the pinnacle of the current AI wave and come to symbolize it in the same way the mobile phone or the Internet characterized previous eras.

A map of technologies related to AI agents and multi-agent systems as presented in this chapter is provided in Fig. 3.1.

It is interesting to note that several of the above technologies have achieved major breakthroughs over the past 5–10 years. This progress helps explain the strong re-emergence of the AI agent field in the current timeframe.

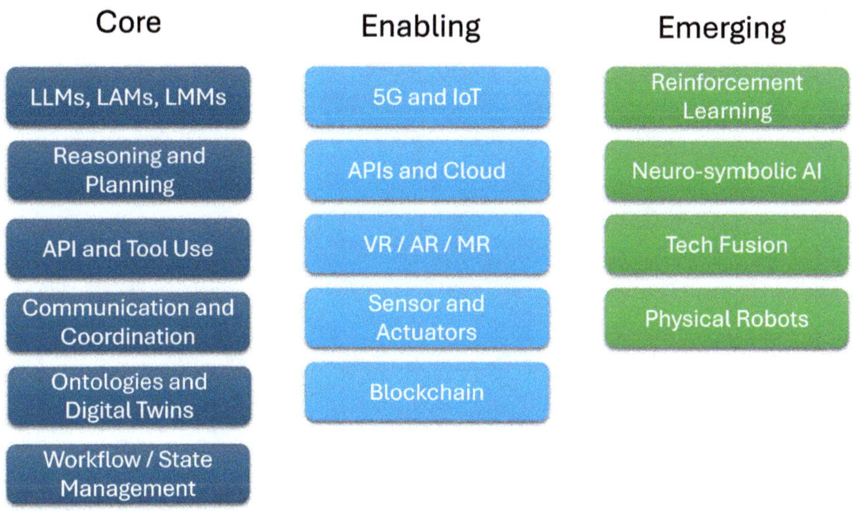

Fig. 3.1 A map of technology areas related to AI agents and multi-agent systems

Chapter 4
Developing Multi-Agent Systems for Autonomic Business

As AI agents gain adoption, business activities shift away from pure innovation and experimentation into how someone can go about designing a multi-agent system (MAS) to start applying autonomic business concepts at scale in the enterprise. We devote this chapter to the key principles of designing multi-agent systems and the inner workings of AI agents. This part of the book is intended for a more technically minded audience, so readers who prefer to focus on value and potential applications may choose to skip ahead to the next chapter.

C. Voudouris, *Autonomic Business Transformation*, Management for Professionals, https://doi.org/10.1007/978-3-032-01415-3_4

4.1 Deciding Your AI Agents

Key concept in designing a multi-agent architecture is to determine the different roles that agents will play within the system and how they will collaborate to achieve the goals of the users and stakeholders involved in the specific enterprise domain [132]. In the design process described below, we draw upon methodologies from legacy agent-building toolkits such as ZEUS [40, 41] and JADE [39], which offer a more robust foundation for agent modelling compared to many contemporary AI agent toolkits, which are still evolving in this regard.

Following the logic of assigning an agent to orchestrate a process, the question arises of how individual activities and tasks can be modelled by agents or how stakeholders and users in the process may be modelled by agents too. The MAS designer would need to identify such candidate entities in an enterprise domain that would make appropriate agents to model sub-tasks, sub-services, and actors within an enterprise-level process. To determine which agents should be created, we must first understand how the application domain is divided, particularly in relation to the roles of the actors within it.

One approach is to create an agent for each role, such as agents to interact with specific types of users or agents to provide task-specific expertise. However, just because agents offer a means of distributing an application does not mean that activities should be distributed as widely as possible. In fact, it is often more efficient to centralize certain activities through systemic or utility agents, which are developed to provide centralized services to other agents within the multi-agent architecture similar to a shared-services function in a real business.

Additionally, agents are often distinguished from other software systems by their ability to interact intelligently with other agents and human users. In a multi-agent system, resources and services may not be directly accessible but are invoked by requesting access through the agent responsible for their control.

The purpose of this is to help separate resources from the entities that will use them to provide services. This is particularly relevant in domains where agents may serve as interfaces to third-party systems and external resources and services, including access to large language models (LLMs). Therefore, specific sources of information, specialized services, or domain expertise often make a good choice for agents when creating a MAS design.

Ultimately, individual actor roles in a business process do not necessarily need to be modelled as individual agents and it is more likely the case that they are combined into single agents. The specific parts or responsibilities that persons, systems, or organizations play in a process are essentially grouped together and performed by a single agent.

4.2 Individual Agent Architecture

Once the set of agents to be designed is clearly defined, and the roles and collaboration models are established, we will proceed with elaborating the Agent Architecture. This involves designing the individual agents and detailing the specific capabilities required for each under the following general functionality areas/modules.

4.2.1 Coordination Engine and Communication Protocols

This module makes decisions concerning the agent's goals based on requests received from humans or other agents. Inputs can be text, multimodal, or, in more structured domains, may follow specific communication languages or protocols. In most current settings, one may assume that an agent is dealing with one request at a time, but in the general case and for long-running tasks, there is a requirement for an agent to handle several requests simultaneously (e.g. invocation of the same business process for several different customers). The coordination engine may have access to information about the agent itself, such as profile and role information, including the service(s) the agent can provide, as well as information about other agents in the multi-agent system and the service(s) they can offer.

Given a request in a certain protocol, the coordination engine could resort to predefined or previously learned behaviours, such as engaging in negotiations with other agents using techniques like contract-net [133] to fulfil the request. In more uncertain cases, it may pass the request to the Reasoning module to set goals or make decisions on how the specific requests can be fulfilled.

Protocols such as Agent2Agent from Google, ACP from IBM or Cisco's AGNTCY should help provide interoperability across different agent platforms and implementations. This space of AI agent communication protocols is what is attracting enormous interest in the current phase, as discussed in Sect. 3.2.3. This is to be expected, since they are building toward the equivalent of "TCP/IP" to underpin the future of multi-agent AI.

Different technologies can be utilized to implement a coordination engine, including graph-type or workflow-type logic that keeps an internal state of interactions with the external environment, directly calling a Retrieval-Augmented Generation (RAG) pipeline or utilizing an LLM, embedded within a reasoning module as explained below, to formulate a response.

4.2.2 Reasoning

This module engages in an intelligent thought process to formulate a response that satisfies a given request. Outputs can be decisions for certain actions (e.g. producing a text output that answers a question) or, in more complex situations, setting the goal(s) to be achieved to satisfy the request. For each goal, the reasoning module may plan a set of actions or delegate this to a dedicated planner and scheduler module specialized in implementing specific goals or decisions made by the reasoner.

Depending on the situation, the reasoning module may hand back control to the coordination engine, providing a set of goals to be achieved externally or a response to be returned to the user (or requesting agent) if the service request cannot be fulfilled. The reasoning module can be implemented in several ways. Key inferencing techniques include:

Neuro-symbolic reasoning: Chain of Thought (CoT) [104], Tree of Thought (ToT) [134], ReAct [105], Q* framework [135].

Probabilistic reasoning: Fuzzy logic [136], Bayesian reasoning [137].

Symbolic reasoning: Logic Programming (LP) [138], Constraint Logic Programming (CLP) [139], Case-Based Reasoning (CBR) [140], knowledge graphs [141].

These inferencing techniques can be underpinned by one or more cognitive models (mostly LLMs with current agents but expandable in future), such as:

Neural network models: Large language models and their variations such as small language models (SMLs) [142], large Action models (LAMs) [118, 119], large multimodal models (LMMs) [143], large reasoning models (LRMs) [144], large cognitive models (LCMs) [145].

Digital models: Digital twins [115], simulation models.

Mathematical models: Weather, molecular, etc.

Additionally, the system may possess short-term memory or long-term memory functionality to improve its reasoning effectiveness and provide context to specific requests (e.g. a personal agent capturing a person's preferences).

4.2.3 Planning and Scheduling

If the agent possesses a dedicated planning and scheduling module, it can refine any goals or decisions taken by the reasoning module to formulate a more detailed set of steps or workflows for execution. In a programmatic implementation of this module, there may be databases of ready-made plan/task templates instantiated to achieve specific goals using standard notations or languages like BPML/BPMN [146]. Alternatively, the system may employ symbolic techniques such as partial order planning [106] utilizing the Planning Domain Definition Language (PDDL) [147] to derive a set of steps instead of a predefined workflow.

In a more agentic scenario involving LLMs, the planner and scheduler may be the same module as the reasoner or a separate module. This module would access one or more of the agent's cognitive models and inferencing techniques to attempt different actions or paths to achieve the desired goals or implement decisions.

In contrast, in a more complex environment such as a factory or fleet management scenario, a dedicated scheduler module may be required to assign tasks to resources (e.g. humans, robots, equipment, other resources) for execution. Other branches of AI such as Constraint Logic Programming have proven quite successful in tackling complex real-world scheduling problems [148]. Essential to this module is orchestrating the set of actions that lead to the desired outcome or goal, as well as replanning or rescheduling as required in case of resource failures also known as dynamic scheduling [149].

4.2.4 Task Execution

This module is crucial for carrying out the steps or tasks determined by the reasoning module and detailed by the planning and scheduling module. Depending on the agent's available skills and tools (internally or externally through protocols such as MCP [49]), various perception (task input) or action (task output) activities can be performed:

Interfaces: Text or multimodal input/output.

Programmatic tools: APIs, components, databases, code generation, code execution, computer/browser use, classic/agentic RPA.

Embodiment (in case of robotics): Sensors, actuators, motors.

During task execution, observation and feedback are often essential to integrate the results of the action on the environment.

4.2.5 Learning

Lastly, the agent may also be equipped with a learning module. This module can enhance the agent's inference logic and cognitive models to improve performance or learn how to achieve goals using either supervised (e.g. causal graphs [150]) or unsupervised learning techniques (e.g. reinforcement learning [128], long short-term memory (LSTM) [151]).

4.3 Creating an Ontology for Agents

To implement AI agents, we must provide (or define, if it's a new domain) the domain ontology: the declarative knowledge that represents the significant concepts, attributes, and values within the specific application domain, as well as the relationships between them. If work has already been done on the data platform and a harmonized data model with well-defined semantics across the organization, the source of the ontology will be in place in the form of a data glossary (business definitions), data dictionary (data specifications), and data catalog (metadata about data assets). For new domains, this harmonized data layer would need to be developed following standard data modelling approaches. It will often involve the identification of the following:

The key entities within the enterprise domain and their relationships.
The attributes of each entity and the types of each attribute.
Constraints or functional relationships between the attributes.

The significance of an entity is easily assessed: if meaningful interaction cannot occur between agents without both parties being aware of it, then the entity is significant and must be modelled. The ontology can be a shared resource across the multi-agent system and may simply provide access to the underlying data platform and associated data glossary, data dictionary, and data catalog, with specific data assets acting as context for the LLM or other advanced cognitive models (LAM [118, 119], LMM [143], LRM [144], LCM [145]) deployed by the AI agent to reason on incoming requests.

Enterprise knowledge is a key component of AI agents. A good knowledge management approach should incorporate mechanisms for knowledge curation, a semantic layer to define relationships between data elements, and standardized definitions to ensure consistency.

The internal architecture of a fully fledged AI agent as explained in this chapter is depicted in Fig. 4.1.

4.4 Implementation and Deployment

During the implementation stage, we will select the appropriate frameworks, tools, and models for developing the MAS architecture and individual agents, possibly favouring rapidly evolving open-source tools and models (e.g. LLMs, low-code tooling, agent frameworks). In the agent instantiation phase, individual agents will be configured to fulfil their process or task-specific responsibilities. Additionally, a configurable template will typically be populated for each agent to capture the agent abilities, role, collaboration models, and position in the multi-agent organization hierarchy.

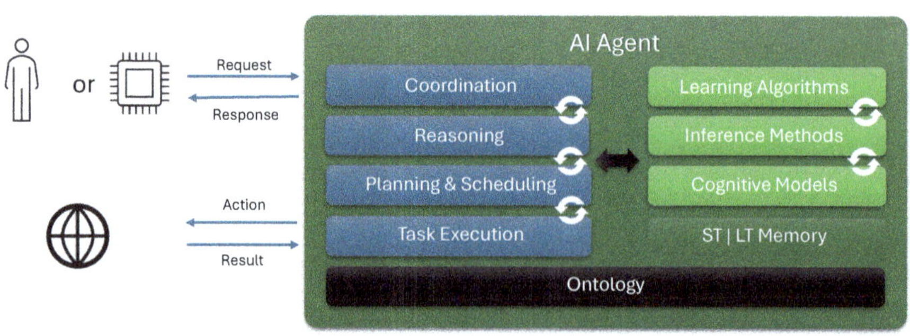

Fig. 4.1 The internal architecture of a fully fledged AI agent

Further work may be needed for systemic or utility agents that provide support services to the ecosystem (see Chap. 10 for concrete examples). The number and nature of these agents will be determined during the project, based on the support needs for operating the agent MAS architecture or in some cases provided by the agent toolkit containing predefined agents capturing key systemic capabilities essential to the architecture.

4.4.1 Demonstrating Trustworthiness

As with other software domains, each agent must be tested independently to ensure it behaves as expected and it is trustworthy. Given the stochastic nature of AI models and the need for continuous agent learning in certain parts of the MAS architecture, a simulation environment can also be developed to perform extensive testing. This ensures agent behaviours meet defined metrics and objectives under varying conditions and input parameters. Testing the interaction and communication between agents within the same simulation environment will allow for end-to-end integration and testing. Statistical techniques can be deployed to ensure observed variability is within acceptable bounds, similar to assessing autonomous vehicle safety with a certain degree of statistical certainty.

4.4.2 Trialing the Integrated Solution

Based on the simulation results, one or more real-world scenarios can be clearly identified, formulated, and targeted for trials. These scenarios should represent the expected use of the multi-agent platform from the end users' perspective. The multi-agent platform and its components will be customized to cater to the selected trial scenarios. This involves using the MAS platform to model detailed domain processes and desired user interfaces, customizing and finalizing these processes and interfaces to suit the solutions being trialled.

A comparative and in-depth analysis of the trial results will typically follow, aiming to identify areas where the services and/or platform require improvements, while highlighting their key benefits and limitations. The evaluation should not be limited to technical and usability issues but should also focus on a socio-economic assessment of the MAS to support wider AI agent adoption within the enterprise. Through typical agile approaches [152], the project team will iterate on the MAS architecture and solution, while driving ever-increasing process and task scope within the domain, embedding the multi-agent system within the business.

4.5 Agent Frameworks and Toolkits

Below, we examine the latest frameworks and toolkits that support the implementation of multi-agent systems as described in this chapter. The area is currently very active, so this list is not exhaustive and represents a snapshot of the most popular frameworks and toolkits at the time of writing.

Despite the emergence of several agentic models and frameworks, the majority focus on the LLM aspect, with multi-agent capabilities still developing. There is, of course, the older generation of agent toolkits and frameworks, such as JADE [39] still popular within the academic community, but these lack the LLM integration that drives the current agentic wave. In terms of modelling multi-agent systems, the following toolkits and frameworks currently stand out.

4.5.1 CrewAI

CrewAI is a Python framework designed for developing multi-agent systems [153]. It aligns well with the concept of roles for agents as explained in this chapter. Tasks are performed by the agents or delegated to other agents, and they retain context within a workflow, enabling the execution of more complex processes. The platform is fully customizable but requires programming expertise, rather than being a visually driven agent design environment.

4.5.2 Autogen, Semantic Kernel, and Magnetic-One

Microsoft has offered three flavours of multi-agent related tools or frameworks [154–156]. Magnetic-One is the primary multi-agent concept, featuring an orchestrator agent that collaborates with several utility agents, including:

Websurfer agent: Performs web tasks

Filesurfer agent: Navigates files and directories

Coder agent: Writes code

Computer terminal agent: Executes line commands for the Coder Agent to generate software

The roles of these agents are relatively fixed, and they operate within the Microsoft Semantic Kernel infrastructure. As the name implies, Semantic Kernel facilitates the integration of LLMs, such as GPT-4, into agents. AutoGen Studio, a low-code tool built into Magnetic-One, provides a visual drag-and-drop interface for building workflows.

4.5.3 LangGraph

LangGraph is designed for building agents with stateful properties, which are essential for handling complex requests and long-term interactions [158]. As the name implies, a graph model is used to orchestrate workflows. LangGraph Studio, a visual tool, is provided for prototyping and deploying agents, while LangSmith completes the toolset and is used to monitor performance.

LangGraph was developed by the same team that created the popular LangChain framework, which helps integrate LLMs into applications. However, LangChain alone is not sufficient, as it can only model simple linear workflows and is therefore unable to handle long-running multi-agent interactions.

A similar concept of using a graph model for coordination and reasoning was also adopted by the ZEUS toolkit [40].

4.5.4 OpenAI Swarm

This is Open AI's take on multi-agent systems [159]. It is based on a stateless approach where agents hold roles and include internal functions but also have the ability to hand off conversations and delegate tasks to other agents based on the conversation flow.

The framework is called experimental and although it is simple to use the lack of state information limits its applicability to the design and architecture principles described in this chapter.

4.5.5 IBM BeeAI

This open-source platform developed by IBM aims to enable developers to run popular open-source AI agents from different frameworks and build their own [160]. Support for multi-agent systems builds on the ACP protocol discussed earlier in the book [113], which currently uses MCP's Anthropic [49], although it is expected to become independent soon.

Initial versions of the platform were based on visual low-code tools geared towards business users. However, the latest iterations have pivoted more towards the developer community. Through BeeAI and ACP, IBM is clearly hoping to attract developers and move towards producing and managing a more universal MAS standard.

4.5.6 Amazon BedRock Agents

AWS's flagship generative AI product BedRock has also introduced multi-agent collaboration features with BedRock Agents [161]. A supervisor agent guides specialized agents to contribute their expertise to a larger workflow by focusing on specific tasks. The supervisor agent can route simple requests directly or, in complex situations, break down the problem and delegate sub-tasks to 'subagents' as needed.

4.5.7 Google Agent Development Kit (ADK)

Last but not least Google's Agent Development Kit (ADK), introduced in April 2025, is a comprehensive framework for managing the lifecycle of single- and multi-agent systems [269]. Built with compatibility in mind, it is both model-agnostic and deployment-agnostic, aiming to bring the familiar experience of software development into agent development.

In terms of support for developing multi-agent systems, various types of agents can be composed such as:

- LLM Agents: AI agents powered by an LLM
- Workflow Agents: Coordination agents designed to orchestrate the execution of flows by their sub-agents.
- Custom Agents: Allowing to develop arbitrary non-LLM logic and build complex workflows as described in this chapter.

Considering the capabilities of previous generations of agent toolkits for multi-agent modelling, developed around the FIPA standards [31], there is still much to be desired from the latest generation of LLM-based agent toolkits. However, given the popularity of the topic and significant efforts by leading tech companies, this gap is expected to close soon.

Chapter 5
Autonomic Business in the Real World

Autonomic business is not a distant vision; examples of it already exist in today's businesses. In this chapter, we will explore these examples and provide insights into where the business opportunities to apply autonomic business (AB) are today. It is crucial for executives to understand AI agents and where they can add value to the business. While one may initially associate operational efficiencies with autonomic business, the most significant benefits in the long run will come from the changes to the business model that AI agents can effect.

C. Voudouris, *Autonomic Business Transformation*, Management for Professionals, https://doi.org/10.1007/978-3-032-01415-3_5

5.1 Agentic Customer Service

One area where business opportunities exist is customer service automation. This area has seen the introduction of chatbots over the past few years, which, together with RPA, has given rise to the concept of hyper-automation [162]. However, the experience has not been satisfactory, with chatbots often unable to answer customer questions and RPA proving brittle to interface and process changes in the business. The promise is that AI agents will change this with their generative AI reasoning and language capabilities.

With OpenAI introducing ChatGPT, the opportunity to replace chatbots with AI agents became more tangible for businesses. One of the early adopters making headlines is Klarna, a financial services company. Their case has been described in several recent announcements, which we will summarize below [163, 164].

Klarna's AI agents have been handling around two-thirds of customer service chats, performing the equivalent work of 700 full-time agents with customer satisfaction scores comparable to human agents. Furthermore, they report improvements in customer resolution times and a drop in repeat inquiries. While some may debate the improvement statistics, there are tangible aspects such as the ability of AI agents to operate 24/7 and communicate in more than 35 languages, which is indisputable. The cost to source similar human language skills and operate them in a 24/7 setup would have been substantial. The AI agent is accessible within the company's mobile app shown in Fig. 5.1.

In addition to customer service support, the company has introduced another AI agent in the form of a shopping assistant, offering a chat-based shopping experience. This assistant helps users spend less time and supports them in finding the right goods at the right price. The AI assistant provides personalized product

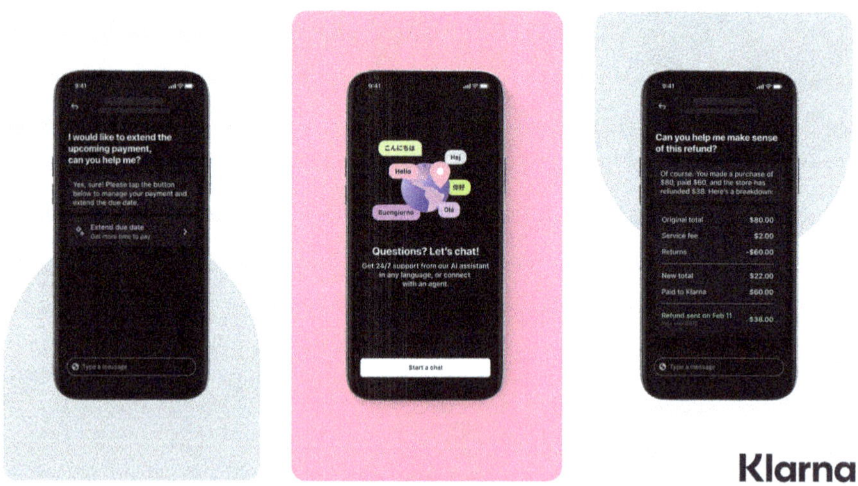

Fig. 5.1 Klarna's AI agent focusing on customer service and issue resolution. *Source*: Klarna

recommendations, expert advice, category and brand comparisons, and access to customer reviews as shown in Fig. 5.2.

While these are straightforward examples of how generative AI can power AI agents interfacing with customers, an even more interesting development at Klarna was the announcement by their CEO [165] that they will be shutting down some of their SaaS applications, such as Salesforce and Workday, in favour of a lightweight stack supported by AI. Later in this chapter, we will explore how these strategies may work architecturally, but it is fascinating to see Klarna contemplating such an approach despite the early phase in the development of mature AI agent solutions to replace the SaaS layer and absorb its business logic. This may seem counterintuitive at first, but ultimately, the logic of AI agents moves us in this direction, as highlighted by remarks from Microsoft's CEO, who also predicted the end of SaaS [166].

5.2 Robotic EV Factory

The real impact of AI agents will be in the physical world when the embodiment of AI systems is achieved. An early example of this can be found in robot-heavy factories. Digital twins and Business Operating Systems, which we will explore later in the book (see Chap. 8) as architectural options to orchestrate robotic operations, are already utilized in such environments.

One example is Hyundai's next-generation EV factory in Singapore [167]. The factory utilizes 200 robots, which perform 50% of all tasks. It is an excellent showcase of how humans, robots, and AI systems can work in harmony in a human-centric environment. AI agents can take the form of physical robots or intelligent systems, as seen in Hyundai's EV factory (→ Fig. 5.3).

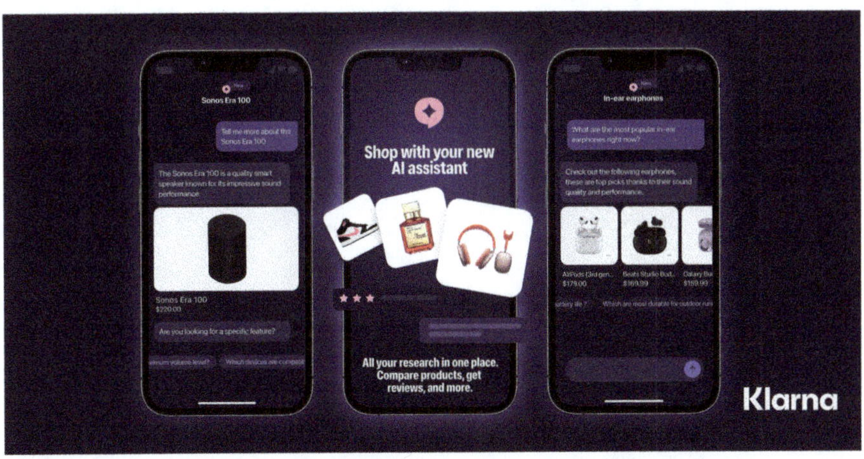

Fig. 5.2 Klarna's AI agent acting as a shopping assistant. *Source*: Klarna

Fig. 5.3 Hyundai's robotic automotive factory in Singapore. *Source*: Hyundai Motor Group Innovation Center Singapore (HMGICS)

Humans and robots work together to install parts on EV cars, such as crash pads and rear bumpers. The entire car body is moved by automated guided vehicles, while inspections are largely automated. Robots handle more than 60% of component process management, ordering, and transportation.

Operating as a digital twin Meta-Factory, the facility synchronizes the virtual and physical worlds in real time. Employees can simulate tasks in the digital virtual space while robots physically move components on the production line. This concept is gaining momentum, with other manufacturers like BMW also creating digital twins of their factories to assess what-if scenarios [168].

Today, humans use the digital twin to assess these options, but this foundation can pave the way for AI to use digital twins as its core cognitive model to test and validate different scenarios, improving operations driven by reasoning techniques such as LLMs.

5.3 Automatic Train Operations

One domain that has advanced significantly in autonomous operations is the railways. Similar to autonomous vehicles, the industry has developed standards for higher degrees of automation. GoA4, or unattended operations, is the highest level, allowing for automatic train protection for safety, driving, route setting, and ensuring timely operations [61]. The system takes over responsibilities for speed, driving, acceleration, braking, collision avoidance, emergency detection, and response using sensors and AI-based incident management. There is no requirement for drivers, attendants, or other staff to be on board for safe operations, although they may be present for other reasons such as customer service. Several lines worldwide are currently operating at the GoA4 level with the latest one being the Thessaloniki Metro line in Greece which opened in late 2024 [169].

Operating systems with high degrees of automation in unattended mode is a significant achievement, especially when applied beyond the metro environment into main railways. The Netherlands' national rail company NS, together with the Spanish train manufacturer CAF, recently and successfully ran an autonomous train near the Dutch city of Groningen, with the vehicle coupling and detecting obstacles without a driver [170] (→ Fig. 5.4).

With railways being one of the most safety-critical domains for applying automation at these levels, we can learn a lot about how to approach risk assessment and ensure the design of safe autonomic systems. One methodology applied in the design of these complex digital railways is the *System of Systems* approach [171]. In Chap. 9, we will explore in detail how a System of Systems approach can be useful in the context of risk assessing complex autonomic business models and operations.

Fig. 5.4 Automatic Train Operation (ATO) is able to detect dummies on the track and stop the train automatically. Image property of CAF

5.4 Autonomous Retail Stores

AI is enabling a significant transformation in retail with the emergence of various autonomous store concepts. This takes the idea of a traditional vending machine and applies it to the entire store, making the shopping experience even more stress-free and frictionless.

In an autonomous store, customers can enter, browse, and shop without the friction of waiting in line, scanning items, or paying at a terminal (→ Fig. 5.5). A prime example is Rewe's autonomous supermarket in Hamburg, Europe's largest, with a surface area of 1200 m^2 [172]. The solution is based on a 3D model of the supermarket that digitally maps its surroundings and movements. Similar to other digital twin models, it allows the system to track purchases and charge only for items taken by customers. Due to data privacy concerns regarding facial recognition, such systems minimize any customer images captured. The technology can be used alone or combined with other sensors to improve the accuracy of computer vision.

Despite some earlier abandoned efforts by Amazon in this area [173], it seems a new wave of solutions with improved algorithms and sensors is emerging. Companies like Rewe and others are investing more in the technology to realize the vision of autonomous stores.

Fig. 5.5 Autonomous stores gain traction with 'pick and go' sections getting introduced. *Source*: REWE

5.5 Autonomous Telecom Networks

Telecoms have long envisioned automating their network operations to the extent that no human intervention is required to keep their core networks running. This vision has gradually come to fruition over the past few years. TM Forum coordination standards in this space recently published a specification for Level 4 (L4) autonomous networking [174], which assumes operators apply AI agents to ensure that the network makes decisions based on awareness information and instructs modules to take further actions without manual interventions. This includes network self-optimization and self-healing with minimal human intervention. As these agents are created, further phases of multi-agent operations and distributed decision-making will follow.

Although there were no examples of L4 networks until recently, this is no longer the case. Tsinghua University in Beijing reported that it began operating its network in autonomous mode in September 2024 [175]. This is a non-profit network with 16,000 nodes. However, this is not the only case; China Mobile also recently announced that it will activate its L4 network serving over 1 billion users in 2025 after completing an L4 trial in an area with over 100 million users [175]. Operating a network of that scale at L4 is unprecedented. The underlying solution involves an AI model supporting 10 billion parameters, including several smaller AI/ML predictive models, along with the ability to simulate scenarios to support automated decisions.

5.6 Financial Services Robo-Advisors

Financial services have been benefiting from autonomic business (AB) models for years. Although not explicitly called agents, human wealth managers have been using automated portfolio allocation since the early 2000s. Clients had to employ a financial advisor who used the software to leverage this capability. This all changed in 2008 when Betterment and Wealthfront released the first so-called robo-advisors [176]. At the core of these early-generation agents was a mathematical framework for crafting a portfolio that maximizes returns for a given risk level.

Generative AI has given another boost to this concept with AI now incorporated in advisory workflows with clients in places such as Morgan Stanley where AI assistants can be used to provide insights to human advisors, facilitate note-taking, and streamline aspects of client meetings. It is easy to foresee LLM technologies and assistants integrated more and more with robo-advisory mathematical models and live market data to substitute the work of human advisors. This may not be desirable in all segments of this industry especially where a deep understanding of client needs and a high degree of trust are required. In Fig. 5.6, we present a possible evolution for robo-advisors inspired by a technology roadmap proposed by Deloitte

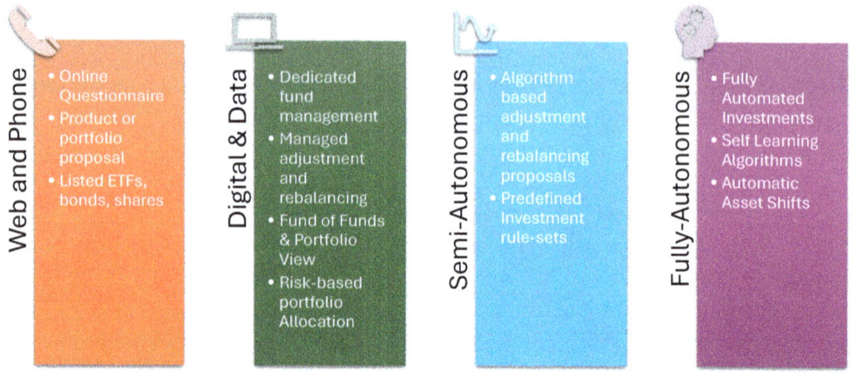

Fig. 5.6 Roadmap for evolution of robo-advisors

back in 2018 [177]. To our knowledge, fully autonomous robo-advisors as shown in the figure are not widely available as of today.

Fraud prevention is another area where pattern matching and machine learning have been used for years processing multi signals to decide if a transaction represents a risk and be potentially fraudulent. Similarly, mortgage applications have been scored by specialized algorithms to aid human decision-making. Again, there is strong foundation to create a largely autonomic business since the mathematical logic and frameworks pre-exist so it is more the case of AI agents completing the picture by orchestrating workflows and automating further customer interactions.

5.7 Further Real-World Examples

Autonomic business models are starting to develop in several other areas. Examples include autonomous farming, with M&S conducting real-world trials [178], robotaxi companies like Waymo reaching nearly mainstream status [179], and autonomous warehouse robotics introduced by companies such as Amazon [180] and Nokia [181]. Additionally, industries like autonomous delivery [182], bus services [183], and shipping [184] are experimenting with autonomous operations, even if they haven't fully developed autonomic business models yet. AI-assisted diagnosis is making inroads in healthcare while transport companies have been using with success AI or operations research algorithms to improve routing of vehicles and management of inventories.

A common trend among these examples is the development of advanced technologies, drawing on AI, digital twins, robotics, and data and analytics. These technologies are reaching levels where they can be successfully integrated into production-quality systems that can operate even in critical safety environments, up to Level 4 on the autonomic scale. This allows for the automation of tasks and processes previously performed or coordinated by humans, now to be managed by intelligent systems.

These intelligent systems possess cognitive models to reason and make decisions, often utilizing digital models of the real world (e.g. digital twins, simulations) to test and apply their decisions. We already covered aspects of this emerging architecture for intelligent systems in the form of AI agents in the previous chapter.

System of Systems, digital twins, Business Operating Systems, and other modelling approaches are used to create the blueprints for autonomic business and assess its risks. These modelling approaches and others will be explored in Chaps. 8 and 9.

5.8 Where to Focus Your AB Efforts

Drawing on the examples in this chapter, we will outline below some key principles on how to extract maximum value from a transition to autonomic business.

5.8.1 Transform the Core Operations of your Business

It is often the case that AI is applied in support functions rather than the core operations of the business. This type of exercise is typically cost-driven and fails to unlock both revenue and cost-saving opportunities. If we draw on the example of the robotic factory, autonomic train operations, and the autonomous telecom network, all these cases drive an autonomic business transformation to the core of the business rather than making some marginal improvements at the edges. This does not mean that there are no opportunities to streamline operations or reduce costs in support processes which should also be followed up but should not be the main focus and target of an AB transformation initiative.

5.8.2 Prioritize Carefully Your Initiatives

Like other transformation programmes, a list of opportunities across the business would need to be gathered and then evaluated. Typically three areas will not be addressed when evaluating each opportunity:

Value creation potential (not only cost savings but also revenue generation).

Resource requirements (what is the investment required to realize the opportunity).

Implementation risk (this may not only reflect technological risk but also legal or regulatory risks which increasingly apply to AI).

Any high value, low risk, low resource projects are the starting areas to create a foundation for AB and prove to the business that autonomic concepts can work and bring quick value to the business. The financial services example where AI assistants are used to support advisors as quick win brings this consideration to light.

A visual representation of a range of initiatives along the axes described above is depicted in Fig. 5.7. Such a visualization approach can ease prioritization.

5.8.3 Combine Revenue Generation with Cost Reduction

With AI agents there is a unique opportunity to target the technology to opportunities that both generate revenue and reduce cost. The example of autonomous stores as well as the Klarna AI shopping assistant exemplifies this opportunity. New shopping experiences can attract customers be it due to convenience ('pick and go' in the case of autonomous stores) or better personalization and choice (AI shopping assistance experience).

This is then combined with the automation benefits emanating from autonomic business operations with limited human intervention and oversight required. The double effect of both more revenue and reduced costs can make the business hypercompetitive versus other businesses where you can pull one lever but only at the expense of the other.

5.8.4 Be Ambitious and Think Outside the Box

Many business and IT leaders have experienced numerous unsuccessful projects and transformations, making them sceptical or even cynical about the potential of new technologies. They often try to fit new projects and proposals into familiar

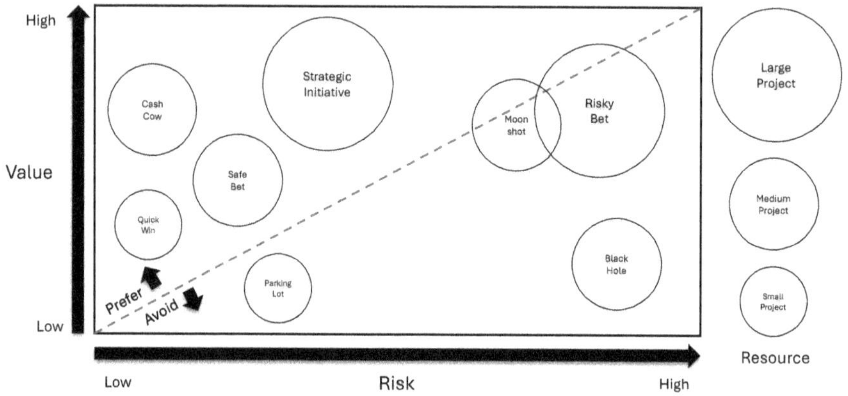

Fig. 5.7 A simple mapping of initiatives against their value, risk, and resource profile can ease prioritizing

patterns based on their past experiences regarding speed of progress and likelihood of success. While this approach has the positive aspect of applying past learnings, it also limits their ability to think outside the box and fully leverage what new technologies can enable.

For example, logic may dictate that the existing CRM system needs to be modified to support an agentic operation. A vendor may even try to convince you that this is absolutely necessary. However, more innovative thinking may suggest that agents and generative AI are transformative enough to reconsider many of your CRM and other SaaS applications. Imagine a world where agents execute work on employees' behalf without them having to access a myriad of apps to collect and collate results. This ambitious drive is exemplified by the Klarna case, where they were not afraid to decommission several legacy applications in areas where AI could have a direct impact and provide an adequate substitute for SaaS.

5.8.5 *Act Rapidly and Decisively*

This wave may be faster than the digital one and those missing out in the beginning will have to face a steeper climb and find it difficult to catch up later on. The 'sit and wait' approach that may have worked in previous eras may not work in this case. The huge amounts of investment top-down from big tech and bottom-up from start-ups are bound to close functionality gaps so an autonomic business vision may arrive sooner rather than later [73].

This may lead to hypercompetitive companies start springing up with more force and speed than in the digital era, taking over from overstaffed and legacy tech-loaded incumbents which are unable to transform because they (a) do not trust the new technologies and (b) haven't got the decisiveness for change. The potential for an 'extinction-level event' in the business landscape across industries cannot be ruled out.

So far in the book, we have explored the concepts and technologies behind autonomic business. However, this is only part of the purpose behind this book. The main objective is to help practitioners and executives initiate and manage all aspects of autonomic business transformation. In the second part of the book, we delve into this subject, focusing more on organizational and transformational aspects and less on the technological aspects of this remarkable revolution.

Part II
Autonomic Business Transformation

Chapter 6
Evolving the Team

A pivotal element of the transformation strategy involves embedding autonomic technologies into the core of the business and promoting collaboration between technology and business teams. As AI agents usher in autonomic business, organizations will evolve into AI–human hybrid environments. In these settings, a substantial portion of marketing, sales, operations, and other domains will be driven by machine-based decisions and workflows, with humans taking on roles of oversight and monitoring. This ensures fallback mechanisms are in place, given the complexity of self-managing and self-adaptive systems.

C. Voudouris, *Autonomic Business Transformation*, Management for Professionals, https://doi.org/10.1007/978-3-032-01415-3_6

This journey will unfold in several phases, akin to the introduction and adoption of digital technologies in the previous era. Moreover, the issue of trust is already playing a significant role, which was less prominent in earlier waves. However, not everything is entirely new. Intelligent systems have been allowed to make decisions for several decades. In areas such as transport and logistics, advanced algorithms, some inspired by reinforcement learning such as Guided Local Search developed by the author of this book [185], routinely make routing, scheduling, and task allocation decisions, something that would have been unimaginable 40 or 50 years ago.

6.1 The Introduction Phase

A valuable transitional concept from the digital transformation wave to the introduction of AI is having business technologists champion the use of AI across the organization. Establishing centres of excellence [187] and transformation networks [188] can accelerate the change in legacy enterprise environments. These efforts can be guided by introducing executive-level champions, such as creating the role of a Chief AI Officer.

Drawing from the digital experience and the role of Chief Digital Officers (CDOs), the model is to have this role and capability as a change agent, eventually handing over a transformed enterprise to traditional roles such as the Chief Marketing Officer (CMO), Chief Operations Officer (COO), Chief Technology Officer (CTO), and Chief Information Officer (CIO) once AI technologies are embedded in the business and most of the change work has been completed.

Reflecting on CDOs, most digital programs never fully completed or realized the benefits and outcomes set at the outset with these roles persisting for years even up to the current day. This may be partly due to the vagueness attached to digitization and what it means for a specific business. Despite numerous and valiant attempts to provide clear definitions [189], a disambiguation of what a truly digitally transformed business looks like was never achieved for the average enterprise.

No doubt AI-centred transformations may suffer from the same lack of clarity and will need clear direction and objectives. Later in the book in Chap. 8, we explore how to mitigate this by defining and documenting an autonomic business strategy and architecting change to realize this strategy.

However, it is important to realize that the introduction and initial transformation phase will not be very effective in the long run unless enterprise-wide roles adapt to serve the needs of an autonomic business. Therefore, a Chief AI Officer or a CTO/CIO overseeing the initial introduction of AI and agentic technologies should eventually give way to a comprehensive transformation program that seeks to align enterprise-wide roles to the new reality, rather than trying to guide AI efforts from a single function or role for a prolonged period of time.

Given the accelerated pace of AI, this phase may take between 6-18 months for mid-size firms. In many cases, the limiting factors are more cultural and governance-related, affecting the ability to gather insights quickly and transition to the next phase.

6.2 The Acceleration Phase

The acceleration and real transformation phase will see AI agents more widely deployed, leading to a situation where human-driven and AI-driven activities start to coexist. This hybrid workforce will not emerge immediately, as issues like trust and the effectiveness of new technologies may take time to be addressed in an enterprise-wide context. Even if some technical challenges are overcome, trust issues may linger and will likely require special focus and attention.

Initially, human employees may direct AI agents to perform specific tasks, such as preparing reports and collecting data on behalf of a human user. Gradually, this will evolve into a multi-agent system scenario where personal and system-wide agents collaborate to serve the needs of human users, who will either sit at the perimeter of this multi-agent system or have centralized control of key functions. As the number of agents proliferates, some agents will become more specialized, while others will assume more coordination and decision-making responsibilities. A machine layer is likely to eventually emerge, working mostly or largely autonomously, with humans receiving services from this layer or tasked with the supervision and monitoring of AI agents, and having the ability to override key decisions and activities within the MAS architecture.

At this point, the organizational design will shift to something similar to the example depicted in Fig. 6.1.

This phase will require at least 12 to 24 months in most organizations. The limiting factors will shift toward organizational readiness, challenges in scaling multi-agent systems, establishing trust in AI agents and regulatory clearance, particularly in more sensitive domains.

6.3 The Establishment Phase

Once multi-agent systems gain a foothold in managing complex tasks and processes, the organization will reach the establishment phase of an autonomic business model. Initially, this may only pertain to autonomic operations, but as the agentic economy gains momentum with customers delegating buying decisions to their personal AI agents, it will also extend to presenting an agentic business front-end. This will enable the business to participate in agentic commerce ecosystems, as explored later in this book (see Chap. 10).

A key characteristic of this phase is that internal roles within the enterprise may start to significantly shift from traditional roles. This shift may also apply to the roles of key suppliers and partners to the enterprise.

Let's examine some of the key executive roles and how they need to evolve to support the needs of an established autonomic business model (see Fig. 6.2):

Chief Executive Officers (CEOs)/Chief Commercial Officers (CCOs): Lead the transition to autonomic business by orchestrating an effective and efficient internal and external AI ecosystem designed to realize the enterprise strategy and objectives.

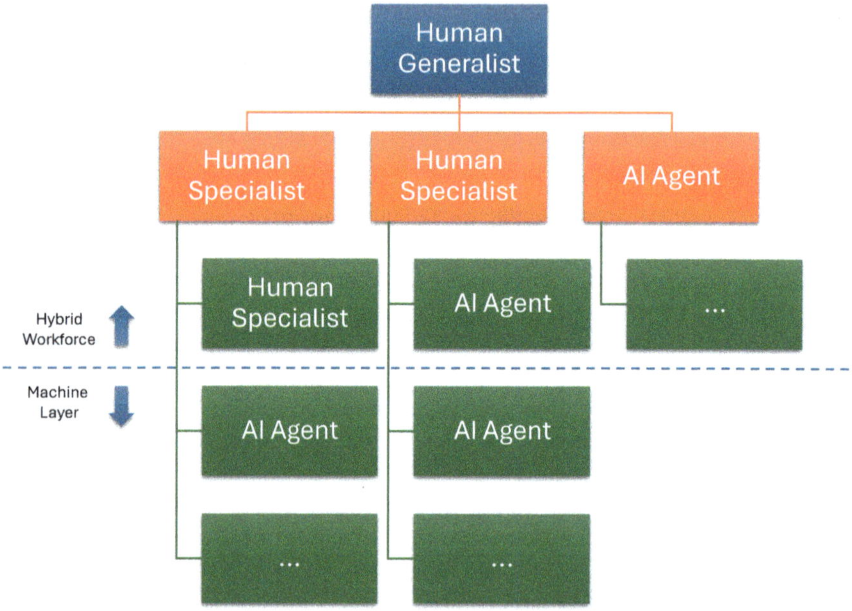

Fig. 6.1 Specialist humans and AI agents working together under human supervision

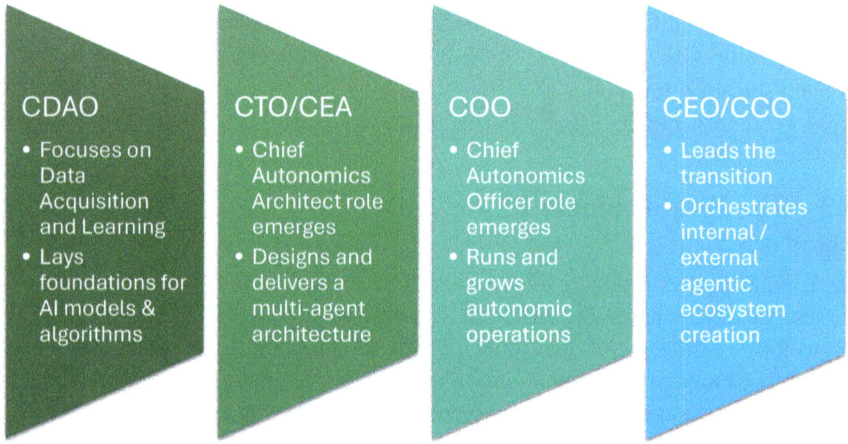

Fig. 6.2 Evolution of key executive roles to support autonomic business

Chief Operations Officers (COOs): Take responsibility for running and growing an organization where autonomic operations are partly or largely in place. The role of *Chief Autonomics Officer* emerges, focusing on directing and monitoring AI-driven or AI-enabled processes and tasks.

Chief Technology Officers (CTOs)/Chief Enterprise Architects (CEAs): Take responsibility for designing and developing a multi-agent architecture that aligns with the company's business processes and value chains. The role of *Chief Autonomics Architect* emerges, replacing or supporting the CTO/CEA.

Chief Data and Analytics Officers (CDAO): Focus on data acquisition and learning, providing the foundations for AI models and algorithms to be customized to the organization's business and operating models.

Throughout the organization, we can also expect changes, with certain departments or functions transitioning to self-managing systems and self-adapting operations run by multi-agent systems. Figure 6.3 illustrates this future where multi-agent systems emerge in the organizational chart, managing entire processes or departments with a mixed human–machine workforce extending to several levels.

The establishment phase may require anywhere between 18 months to 5 years, or even longer, as security, ethical, governance, legal and regulatory challenges and uncertainties take centre stage. The three phases of initiation, acceleration, and establishment of an autonomic business and organizational enablers and changes appearing in each phase are presented in Fig. 6.4. The end-to-end journey across the three phases may take anywhere between 3 years to nearly a decade, or even longer.

6.4 Impact on Employees: What to Expect

Some may argue that a fully-fledged autonomic business model could take several years to materialize. However, given the rapid pace of change and the current investment in maturing AI technologies, a two- to three-year timeframe for

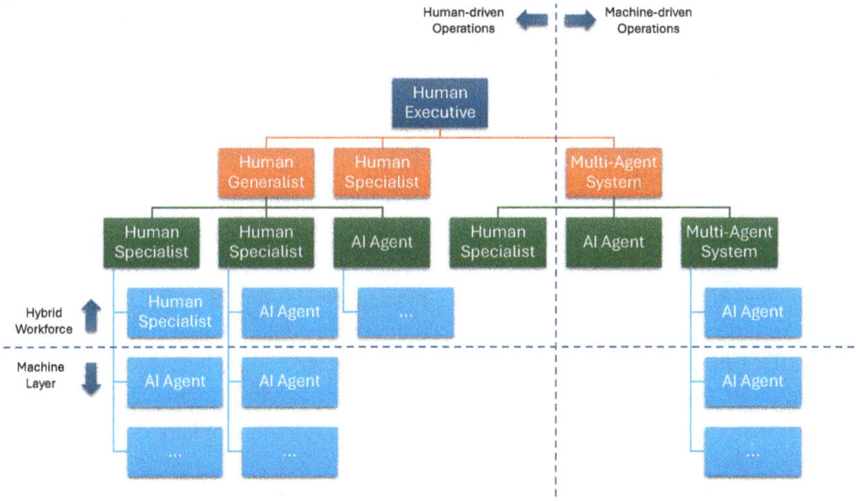

Fig. 6.3 Humans and AI agents working together to achieve complex enterprise objectives

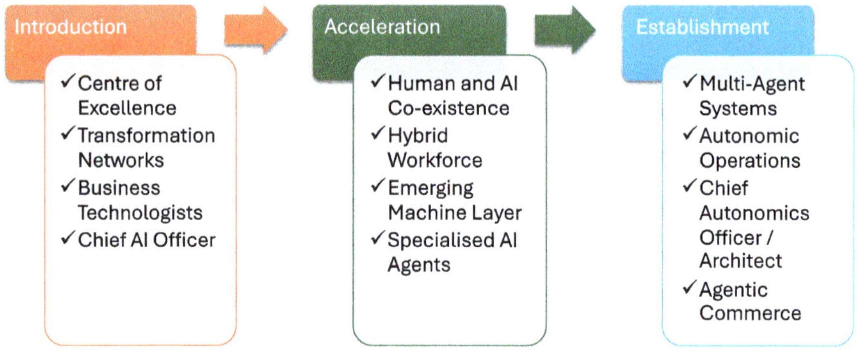

Fig. 6.4 Adoption phases of autonomic business and organizational enablers and changes signifying transition to each phase

realizing a version of a business model that we may recognize as autonomic business may not be too far-fetched. Organizations need to start preparing now for the transition from a largely human-driven enterprise to AI-driven business and autonomic operations. This transition may present more challenges than anticipated. Humans have developed the skills to direct and teach other humans for millennia, but the same cannot be said for interactions between humans and AI agents. Movies such as *2001: A Space Odyssey* provide a glimpse of the difficulties that could arise when humans try to work together with intelligent machines. Nonetheless, there will also be practical challenges, at least in the short term, as the technology can be quite complex and require significant handholding from human operators to deliver the expected results. The burden will most likely be falling on the shoulders of IT departments playing the role of 'HR' for this new army of AI digital workers [259].

There are qualitative differences from past automation efforts and technologies. Systems to date have shown little ability to learn and adapt. Implementing a new ERP or CRM system meant that human users had to learn and adapt to comply with the workflows implemented in these solutions or modify them at significant expense to meet user and enterprise-specific requirements and business flows. AI agents represent a unique opportunity for systems to learn and discover how to achieve goals within a business without adhering to fixed workflows. This provides immense flexibility and potentially removes the need to endlessly customize and support applications to meet human requirements.

However, this does not eliminate the burden of setting the right goals for AI agents and learning how to control them, so they achieve these goals effectively and efficiently. Initially, this may be required at the micro level, where agents perform specific tasks, but later on, at the macro level, where agents are in charge of whole processes and end-to-end flows. The discipline of AgentOps can help in this area, as will be explored in the next chapter.

To understand what a technology-heavy autonomic business environment might look like, we can examine the tech-heavy equivalents of traditional industries, such as fintech, insurtech, and proptech. For example, fintech companies often boast high percentages of technology staff, with cases like Alipay and its parent AntGroup having over 60% of staff dedicated to tech roles [190]. It is not unreasonable to assume that businesses successfully transitioning to an autonomic business model will rely more on business technologists with a heavy focus on understanding AI and agentic technologies. These technologists will monitor and maintain autonomic operations as they are upgraded and customized to meet a rapidly changing external environment increasingly focused on machine-to-machine transactions.

Previous industrial revolutions had a profound impact on employment and societies. One key question is whether autonomic business will lead to widespread unemployment or create opportunities for reskilling. Emerging evidence suggests that employers will prefer employees with AI skills over those without, even if they are less experienced in the specific domain [191]. This preference makes sense in the 'Introduction' phase of autonomic business, as these 'business technologists' will be essential for laying the foundations for what is to follow. As companies move into the acceleration phase, the focus will shift to human–machine collaboration, with employees orchestrating the work of AI agents. Once multi-agent systems can start performing the work of entire teams, the workforce will undoubtedly experience significant disruption.

There will be many challenges along the way. LLM-based AI agents are based on non-deterministic approaches, making them less predictable than rule-based systems or traditional application software. Like new employees, AI agents will require training and oversight, as they are bound to initially make frustrating mistakes. Their behaviour may sometimes appear inconsistent and not aligned with expectations.

Management-level agents may need to be developed to supervise other agents, enforce company policies, reduce errors, and remedy miscommunications with customers. Similar to employee retirement, issues such as transferring AI agent learnings and knowledge to new generation architectures and upgraded AI software may become central to avoid prolonged training and testing of each generation of AI agent technology.

To manage these challenges, new jobs may be created in the economy, similar to the digital giants that emerged from the Internet era, such as Google, Facebook, Amazon, Uber, and Airbnb. These new giants could focus on agentic commerce, becoming brokers or aggregators of agent ecosystems that provide specialized AI technologies to different vertical industries.

Given the pace of innovation and the ever-reducing cost of developing high-performing LLM models (e.g. DeepSeek [95]), one may wonder whether organizations will be fast enough to adopt new technologies ahead of their competitors. Ultimately, agentic AI and multi-agent systems offer the opportunity to create high-performing teams that seamlessly collaborate across organizational boundaries, something long sought after for human teams. Businesses that seize this opportunity may quickly overtake inefficient legacy businesses that stick to their old ways of working.

6.5 Creating a Transformation Blueprint

It is crucial to plan the autonomic business (AB) transformation into a cohesive blueprint that links investment in AI technologies with organizational changes and competitive advantage, considering the external context and environment. Such a blueprint should address four key thematic areas as also highlighted in a recent survey of extracting business value from AI [192]:

AI capability: This area concerns the creation of a robust autonomic business strategy coupled with strong company-wide governance to realize it. This strategy would need to be translated into a fit-for-purpose multi-agent architecture which in its turn will have to be realized deploying suitable AI cognitive models that leverage the organization's data and technology resources.

AI-enabled change: The difficult task of AI-enabled change lies in the core of being able to create value from investments in AI capability development. Systematic process and task automation across the enterprise, followed by decision-making and goal setting automation utilizing a human-led machine workforce, will have to be planned and executed. This implies new roles and organizational capabilities having to be created along with structural changes to align the enterprise to its autonomic business strategy objectives. These objectives will increasingly concern the agentic value proposition towards customers, rather than purely focusing on internal optimization initiatives.

AI value creation: The above changes will have to be reflected in improved financial performance. This may initially come from operational efficiency and improved customer experience but gradually the focus is bound to shift on customer value through agentic ecosystem creation (see Chap. 10). Continuous innovation delivery should underpin all the above areas to lead to sustained enterprise value generation.

Enterprise context and environment: The impact on customers, partners, and suppliers will be profound and if not planned and managed appropriately may hinder internal AI adoption. The enterprise will have to transform its whole ecosystem or pivot to a new ecosystem to realize the full benefits of an AB transformation. External battles with competitors as well as legal and regulatory challenges may be more profound compared to previous transformations. Potential or actual responses from these external actors would have to be assessed, evaluated, and responded.

The linkages between these four thematic areas and their respective sub-topics are illustrated in Fig. 6.5.

6.6 Key Challenges in Autonomic Business Transformation

Any AI transformation, particularly an autonomic business transformation, is expected to face several challenges that may hinder change. Based on the transformation blueprint above, we can highlight seven areas that form a framework for capturing and systematically addressing these challenges:

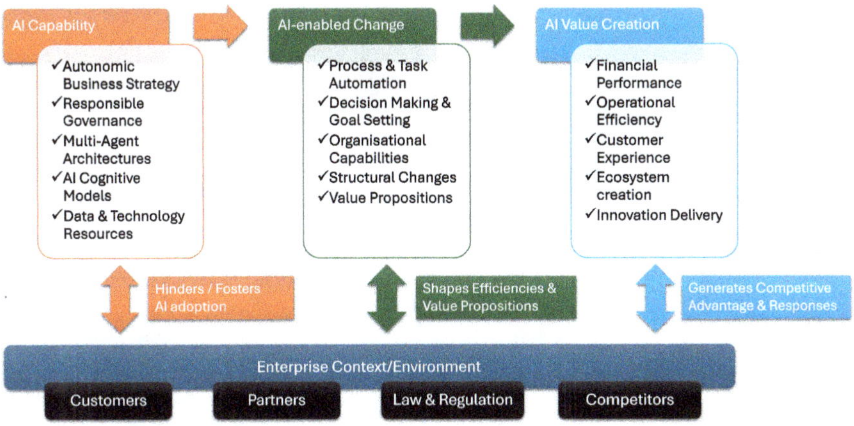

Fig. 6.5 A transformation blueprint for autonomic business

Leadership alignment and support behind a clear and comprehensive AB strategy.

Defining investment in AI resources required to deliver the AB strategy, including securing lead partner and customer participation.

Clear approach to sourcing the prerequisite data and technology foundations to enable AI agents to operate effectively.

Assessment of current process inventory to determine suitability for transitioning to autonomic operations.

Evaluation of current culture in terms of compatibility with the mission and vision of the AI strategy.

Creation of a strong AI business case that does not conflict with existing Digital and Cloud strategies.

Articulation of specific AI benefits that can be readily measured and monitored.

These challenges are not independent but rather interconnected in a circle of reinforcement, as shown in Fig. 6.6. Addressing them leads to an overall improvement in the organization's ability to deploy and leverage AI to create business value [192].

Both the key aspects of the transformation blueprint and the challenges, along with strategies to tackle them, are explored in detail in the following chapters. Before we conclude this chapter on team evolution, it is worth exploring one more concept: how a super small company can become an AI giant by adopting and scaling an autonomic business model.

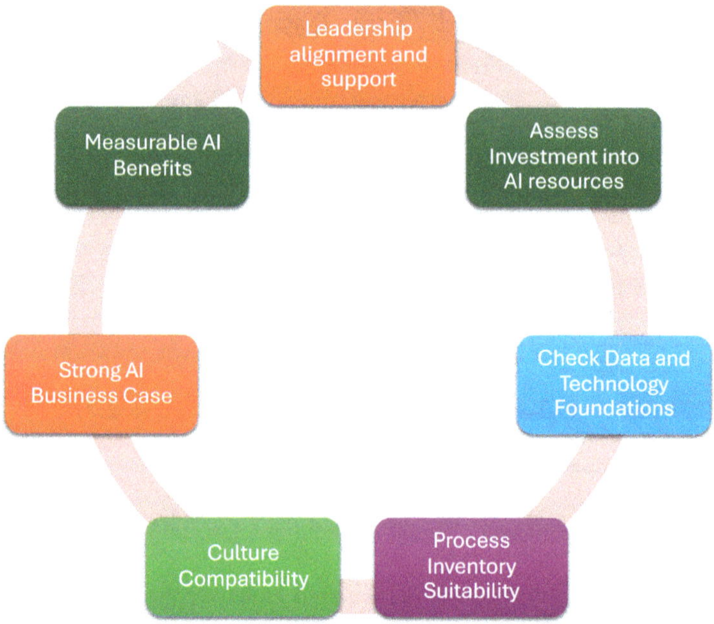

Fig. 6.6 Key challenges to absorb AI technologies and enable autonomic business

6.7 Autonomic Business Singularity

In January 2024, OpenAI's Sam Altman captured headlines with his speculation about the emergence of the world's first one-person billion-dollar company, enabled by advances in AI [193]. Instagram famously had only 13 employees when it was sold to Facebook, setting a precedent for digital giants achieving unicorn status despite low headcount [194]. Imagine what an AI giant could look like in a hypothetical future where business growth using autonomous AI agents becomes uncontrollable and irreversible.

This scenario can be seen as the business equivalent of a singularity, where an upgradable business model enters a positive feedback loop of self-improvement iterations, causing a rapid increase in competitive advantage. This 'black hole' effect could absorb or obliterate all competition in a specific market. Although this is an intriguing idea, it faces certain challenges, such as the ability of others to easily replicate the same business model, creating other similar super-competitive entities. Additionally, market regulations could impose controls to prevent such entities from gaining a dominant position, although slow initial responses by governments may well lead to detrimental impacts. This is similar to how digital giants rapidly dominated e-commerce and social media with regulators playing catchup ever since.

Leaving aside such extreme scenarios, autonomic businesses reaching Level 4 or 5 on the autonomic scale could give rise to companies with very few human employees, scaling through the use of AI agents to become the unicorns of the future, even in traditional sectors and industries. One can imagine a company with 25–50 employees generating $1 billion in revenue or $20–$40 million in revenue per employee, relying largely on multi-agent systems to manage operations and transact with customers and suppliers. Very small teams managing such large organizations would require the emergence of a new kind of human employee with the following characteristics [261]:

Significant knowledge breadth across various functions of the business to oversee and direct the underlying autonomic operations.

Technological understanding of AI and eagerness to follow developments, adopting and integrating the latest AI innovations into the business.

Deep understanding of human and AI collaboration to maximize the benefits of a human-led machine workforce.

These scenarios make it even more important for businesses today to adopt an autonomic business model before AI agents emerge through startups in their respective domains. AI agents will spark a new wave of innovation, with autonomic business concepts starting to emerge and gradually dominate as the next wave after digital business. Changes will be faster than previous waves, and those missing out may face a huge productivity gap and a mountain to climb over the next decade.

Chapter 7
New Capabilities and Challenges

Transitioning to an autonomic business (AB) model necessitates the development of new organizational capabilities while also presenting a unique set of challenges. As a technology-driven transformation, AB does not occur in isolation; rather, it builds upon existing competencies and previously established frameworks. For most

C. Voudouris, *Autonomic Business Transformation*, Management for Professionals, https://doi.org/10.1007/978-3-032-01415-3_7

organizations, the journey towards AB maturity begins with foundational IT standards and best practices, most notably those outlined in the Information Technology Infrastructure Library (ITIL) [195].

Today, ITIL is widely recognized and well understood by IT professionals. Foundational ITIL training has become commonplace, with many IT department staff members completing certification courses to ensure alignment with industry standards. These technology operational practices need to evolve and get extended to cater for the needs of autonomic business.

7.1 Evolution of Technology Operational Practices

ITIL has proven effective for traditional IT environments, where long implementation cycles were typically followed by a transition into steady-state service operations. However, the rise of digital technologies and the widespread adoption of agile methodologies, aimed at accelerating software development, highlighted the need for a more responsive and integrated approach to infrastructure and operations.

This need gave rise to DevOps [196], a methodology that extends agile and lean principles beyond development. DevOps emphasizes automation, collaboration, and continuous integration, enabling organizations to streamline workflows and build infrastructure that supports the continuous delivery of software. By bridging the gap between development and operations, DevOps has become a critical enabler of modern, fast-paced application lifecycles.

As data and analytics gained prominence, a similar evolution unfolded. Inspired by DevOps and agile methodologies, DataOps [197] emerged to bring the same focus on speed, quality, and continuous improvement to data workflows. Rooted in lean principles, DataOps aims to streamline the development and deployment of data pipelines, ensuring they are agile, reliable, and scalable.

As data pipelines expanded beyond traditional reporting, powering real-time insights and automated decision-making, the need to manage the full lifecycle of AI and machine learning (ML) models became apparent. This led to the rise of MLOps and AIOps [198], which apply DevOps-inspired practices to the operationalization of AI/ML.

The objective remains consistent across these evolutions: to define best practices and provide tools that support the end-to-end lifecycle of AI/ML models, enhancing their speed, reliability, and effectiveness in delivering actionable insights and autonomous decisions.

A familiar pattern emerges: each technological shift in software development and operations gives rise to a corresponding set of engineering practices and tools that bridge the gap between innovation and operationalization. These practices consistently aim to improve speed, quality, and automation.

In the context of autonomic business (AB), we can identify two distinct layers of engineering required to support the development and operation of agentic capabilities:

- **Cognitive model engineering:** This layer focuses on the foundational cognitive models, such as large or small language models, which power agentic capabilities across the enterprise. Assuming the use of Retrieval-Augmented Generation (RAG) pipelines [199] and other model workflows, LLMOps / LangOps [200] represent the emerging set of best practices and tools for developing, deploying, and managing these models effectively.
- **Agentic system engineering:** At the level of individual agents and multi-agent systems, there is a growing need for AgentOps [201]—a discipline focused on engineering practices that support the lifecycle management, coordination, and orchestration of autonomous AI agents.

We will explore both LLMOps/LangOps and AgentOps in greater detail in the following sections. The objective remains consistent: to establish best practices and provide tools that support the end-to-end lifecycle of AI/ML models, enhancing their speed, reliability, and effectiveness in delivering actionable insights and autonomous decisions.

7.2 Cognitive Model Engineering: From LangOps to ModelOps

At the heart of recent advancements in agentic technologies is the ability to harness large language models (LLMs) to reason, plan, and execute actions that fulfil specific goals whether defined by human users or initiated by other agents in a multi-agent system. LLMs offer broad cognitive capabilities, enabling them to address a wide range of topics and tasks. However, in enterprise settings, such general-purpose intelligence is not always necessary or even desirable.

In many cases, small language models (SLMs) [142], designed with a narrower focus, are better suited for domain-specific applications. These models not only align more closely with targeted agentic tasks but also offer significant advantages in terms of computational efficiency for both training and inference.

Between these two extremes lies a middle ground: domain-specialized LLMs. These are large models fine-tuned or pre-trained on specific disciplines such as law, science, and mathematics offering deep contextual understanding within a defined scope.

In this context, the foundational layer of agentic systems across the enterprise may rely on a diverse ecosystem of language models, including:

- Frontier LLMs for general-purpose reasoning
- SLMs for lightweight, task-specific operations
- Specialized LLMs for domain expertise

The development and operation of these models, along with the pipelines that prepare inputs and extract outputs, require dedicated engineering practices. This emerging discipline is known as *LLMOps* or *LangOps*. It encompasses best practices and tools for managing the lifecycle of language models, including accuracy validation, deployment automation, and continuous improvement.

We are already witnessing the evolution of *LangOps*, with early tools and frameworks focusing on model evaluation, monitoring, error reduction, and rapid iteration. As a variety of cognitive models are deployed including Large Action and Multimodal Models, this area is likely to evolve into *ModelOps* covering a wide range of AI models underpinning agentic operations.

7.3 Agentic Systems Engineering: AgentOps

Single-agent operations typically evolve around LangOps or ModelOps, which focus on managing the interfaces between an AI agent and its users, other agents, or integrated tools. As the concept of the autonomic business (AB) expands to encompass AI-driven modelling of entire processes and systems, the need arises for more sophisticated architectures, namely multi-agent systems (MAS).

Chapter 8 explores the architectural foundations of MAS in greater detail. From both technological and business perspectives, developing and operating one or more MAS platforms across the enterprise introduces a new level of complexity; one that must be automated, monitored, and continuously improved. These challenges are not unlike those encountered in managing highly distributed systems.

While agent toolkits for building, deploying, and operating MAS are not new, many have been developed over the years, particularly within academic and research communities; these earlier systems were largely rule-based and deterministic. In contrast, today's LLM-powered agents exhibit stochastic behaviour, requiring new approaches to engineering and operations.

Once a solid LangOps or ModelOps foundation is in place to manage the language model or other cognitive model components of agentic functionality, a higher-level operational layer can be introduced to support the distributed development, testing, and live operation of a MAS. This is essential to ensure that agents perform accurately within domain-specific tolerances and meet the trustworthiness requirements necessary for real-world deployment.

Key capabilities in this emerging discipline of AgentOps include [260]:

- Automated MAS creation and orchestration
- Rigorous testing and validation frameworks
- Real-time observability, telemetry, and monitoring
- Continuous improvement and lifecycle management

AgentOps is already gaining traction as a critical enabler in enterprise-scale AI agent services such as those provided by Azure [202]. In the next section, we will summarize all these key *X-Ops* capabilities and map them to the autonomic maturity scale, helping organizations identify which capabilities are most relevant to their current stage of transformation.

7.4 Mapping Capabilities to the Autonomic Scale

Figure 7.1 illustrates how various X-Ops (DevOps, DataOps, etc.) disciplines align with the levels of the autonomic maturity scale.

At Level 0 (Limited Support), foundational IT processes and standards are established through frameworks like ITIL, which provide the baseline for structured IT service management within the enterprise.

Progressing to Level 1 (Human Assistance), the shift towards more agile and responsive development practices becomes essential. This stage introduces DevOps, enabling faster and more reliable application delivery through integrated development and operations toolchains.

As machine capabilities begin to augment human decision-making, Level 2 (Partial Automation) calls for DataOps. This discipline focuses on building robust, scalable data pipelines that support both human insights and automated analytics.

At Level 3 (Conditional Automation), AI/ML models are deployed to automate decision-making processes. This necessitates the adoption of AIOps/MLOps, which ensures the reliable development, deployment, and monitoring of AI/ML models across the enterprise.

Moving into Level 4 (Goal-Oriented Automation), AI agents powered by LLMs begin to assist users not just in decisions, but in setting and achieving goals. Here, LangOps or ModelOps becomes critical for managing a diverse ecosystem of language models, ensuring their accuracy, efficiency, and alignment with business needs.

Finally, at Level 5 (Full Autonomy), agents operate independently across complex processes. This level introduces AgentOps, a discipline focused on the

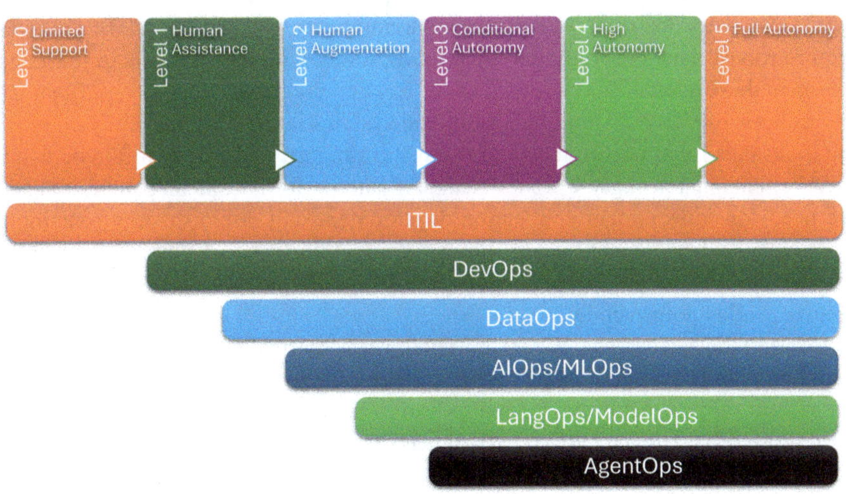

Fig. 7.1 Mapping X-Ops capabilities across the different levels of maturity in the autonomic business scale

orchestration, monitoring, and continuous improvement of multi-agent systems. As autonomy increases, so does the need for advanced AgentOps capabilities to ensure trustworthiness, safety, and performance in live environments.

7.5 How IT's Role Will Change

As autonomic business redefines enterprise operations, the role of IT must evolve along the maturity X-Ops curve, as outlined earlier. This evolution involves transforming and layering new capabilities atop traditional ITIL frameworks. However, this shift presents a significant challenge particularly for organizations that have heavily outsourced their IT functions, leaving them with diminished internal capabilities and a strategic disadvantage.

In this context, organizations face two primary paths forward:

- Insourcing the transformation to build an internal AB capability
- Switching to new providers that specialize in agentic transformation, enabling a shift from an application-centric to an agent-driven operational model

Rather than deploying and maintaining a multitude of applications, the focus will shift towards identifying, sourcing, onboarding, training, and monitoring AI agents. This mirrors the responsibilities of HR departments managing human employees. As such, IT's role is poised to evolve into a kind of agentic HR, overseeing the robotic workforce that powers AB [259].

The transformation of IT infrastructure to support these complex systems will be equally demanding, especially for organizations that have yet to complete their cloud and digital transformations. According to Gartner, by 2028, at least 15% of day-to-day work decisions will be made autonomously by AI agents [203]. This will require robust data and analytics capabilities, along with vast datasets to train and optimize these agents.

Vendors, too, face disruption. Traditional systems integrators, currently employing thousands for application development and support, will face a shift in demand. As AI agents increasingly wrap tools and APIs to perform tasks on behalf of users, the need for conventional application development will diminish. Any remaining work will be heavily automated through generative software development. This necessitates a major pivot, from applications to agents, posing a significant transformation challenge for vendors.

Overall, these changes will reshape enterprises internally and redefine their relationships with IT and technology suppliers. Tech-savvy organizations with insourced capabilities will be better positioned to lead in the autonomic business era. In contrast, those reliant on outsourced IT will need to forge closer partnerships with leaders in agentic AI, potentially phasing out traditional application vendors that fail to adapt.

True autonomic businesses are likely to have up to 70–80% of their workforce in technology roles, with 20–30% of these specializing in AI and data, a clear indicator of the strategic importance of these capabilities in the future enterprise.

7.6 Defining the Roles of the Agentic Architect and Engineer

As the AI agent estate within enterprises continues to expand, the burden on IT and technology staff to provide oversight and assurance will grow significantly. This will drive the emergence of the new specialist roles of agentic architects and agentic engineers tasked with designing and implementing multi-agent systems across the enterprise.

These roles must be highly dynamic and responsive, as multi-agent systems are inherently non-deterministic and may alter their behaviour based on incoming data. Anomalies or cascading errors within such environments may require immediate intervention to preserve operational stability. In some cases, this could even necessitate architectural changes to reroute workflows around degraded components of the system.

Given the critical role of data in shaping AI agent behaviour, the responsibilities of data and analytics professionals will also evolve. Their focus will shift towards:

- Monitoring and validating the performance of autonomous AI agents
- Improving data quality to enhance the accuracy and reliability of agent-driven decisions

To support this new paradigm, enterprises will need to develop next-generation IT support workflows. These workflows should enable both human users and AI agents to report issues as they arise. AI systems may initially triage these issues and apply temporary fixes, escalating more complex problems to human experts, either in agentic engineering or in data analytics, depending on whether the root cause lies in agent functionality, data integrity, or both.

7.7 Data and Learning Foundations

The Internet has often been described as the fossil fuel for training large language models (LLMs) [83], a highly valuable yet finite resource. This limitation constrains the potential of current-generation LLMs and underscores the growing importance of synthetic data, multimodal inputs, simulations, and other generated data sources to sustain future advancements in AI training.

At the enterprise level, internal data and business processes form a critical foundation for AI agents. These agents must learn from and reason within the context of this proprietary information. To support this, organizations will need a robust data platform that brings the enterprise's domain ontology to life.

Establishing such a platform is a foundational step towards enabling an autonomic business. It requires:

- A harmonized data model with consistent semantics across the organization
- A well-defined domain ontology, expressed through:
  - A data glossary (business definitions).
  - A data dictionary (technical specifications).
  - A data catalog (metadata about data assets).

This shared semantic framework enables AI agents to communicate effectively, grounded in a common understanding of enterprise context.

Looking beyond the enterprise, cross-company agentic interactions will demand similar efforts at the industry level. Standardized domain ontologies and interoperable data platforms will be essential for enabling autonomous agents to operate across organizational boundaries, facilitating intercompany transactions and collaborative agentic ecosystems.

The importance of data in underpinning agentic supply chains cannot be overstated. As illustrated in Fig. 7.2, industry- and enterprise-wide domain ontologies, supported by mature data management platforms, will form the bedrock of agentic AI and Autonomic Business.

This is not to suggest that everything must be built from the ground up. Significant progress has already been made through various data standardization and ontology initiatives across industries. Examples include the TM Forum standards in telecommunications [204], HR Open Standards in human resources [205], and the Financial Industry Business Ontology (FIBO) in finance [206], among others.

7.8 Process and Task Foundations

Sitting atop the enterprise data platform is typically a layer of process- and task-specific applications and tools, responsible for orchestrating and automating large portions of business operations.

This process and task layer is poised for a profound transformation with the rise of AI agents. Rather than interacting directly with applications and tools, human

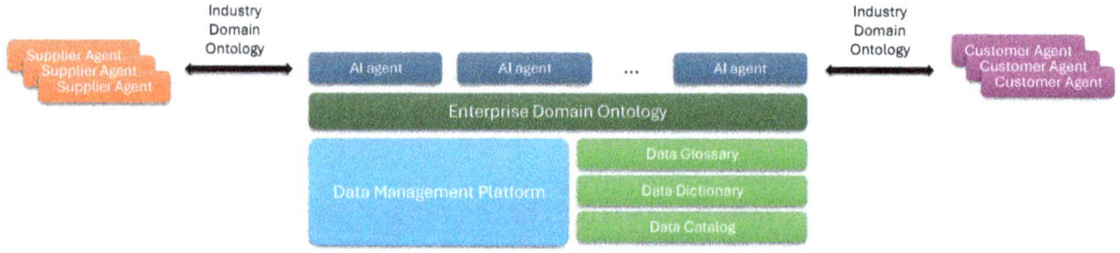

Fig. 7.2 Ontologies and data management platforms will enable internal and external agentic supply chains

users will increasingly delegate tasks to intelligent agents. These agents, leveraging APIs, tools, and browsing capabilities, will autonomously execute the necessary actions to fulfil user-defined goals.

Historically, enterprise automation relied on RPA technologies, which used Optical Character Recognition (OCR) to interpret screen content, some dating back to the mainframe era, and executed scripted, deterministic workflows to automate data entry and routine tasks. While these legacy systems laid the groundwork by capturing key processes and orchestrating workflows, they were limited in flexibility and adaptability.

The next evolution is an agentic RPA, powered by large language models (LLMs) and agentic browsing capabilities, as discussed in Chapter 3 on technology foundations. Unlike traditional RPA, which is rule-based and brittle, LLM-powered agents are context-aware, adaptive, and capable of reasoning in real time.

The key distinctions between LLM-based agents and classic OCR-based RPA are illustrated in Fig. 7.3, highlighting the shift from static automation to dynamic, intelligent task execution [121].

As multi-agent systems are introduced, direct agent-to-agent communication will become increasingly prevalent (see Sect. 2.4). In this evolving landscape, human users will shift towards a supervisory role, focusing on monitoring, oversight, and intervention when necessary, while AI agents take on a growing share of process execution and task automation.

7.9 Validation Verification and Testing

As AI agents take on greater responsibilities within an autonomic business (AB) framework, the need for rigorous validation, verification, and testing becomes critical. Unlike traditional systems that rely heavily on predefined, well-documented

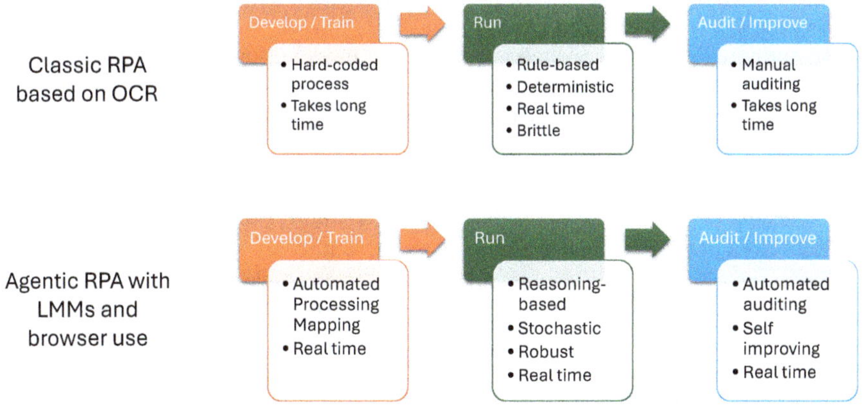

Fig. 7.3 Differences between classic RPA and agentic RPA

processes, agentic systems ideally learn and adapt, absorbing information and process flows through observation, interaction, and discovery.

In this paradigm, the system doesn't just follow the business; it learns how the business operates, identifies opportunities for optimization, and even enhances legacy functionality. This represents a fundamental shift: rather than forcing the business to conform to rigid system constraints (often at high cost), the system adapts to the business, evolving to support and improve it.

7.10 Organizational Sandboxes

Concepts such as the digital twin of an organization and agent-based simulation become essential when creating safe, realistic sandboxes to unlock the full potential of autonomous agents without risking disruption to live operations. These environments allow agents to demonstrate reasoning, cognitive, and decision-making capabilities in controlled settings. Once validated in simulation or through interaction with a digital twin, agents can be more confidently transitioned into real-world deployment.

Simulation environments also serve as training grounds, enabling agents to refine their skills in complex or edge-case scenarios. These environments help agents learn to recognize outliers, adapt to unexpected inputs, and develop robust response patterns. This approach can be extended further by modelling customers, suppliers, or partners through digital twins that reflect their behaviours derived from event data stored in the enterprise's data layer.

Digital twins provide the structural framework to collect and contextualize data across the business ecosystem. They enable agents to learn and reason within specific domains, not only from text and visual data but also from event sequences, actions, and interactions that drive business outcomes. In some cases, agents may even require embodiment, operating in physical environments such as warehouses, factory floors, and offices, mirroring the data-rich learning processes seen in autonomous vehicle development.

To support this evolution, large multimodal models (LMMs) and large action models (LAMs), as introduced in Sect. 3.2.5, will complement LLMs by enabling agents to operate across text, video, and physical action domains. These models form part of a growing cognitive model repertoire, which agents can invoke to perform specialized tasks. Techniques like reinforcement learning help agents learn action sequences to achieve goals, while transfer learning allows capabilities to be shared across agents without retraining from scratch.

Emerging concepts such as large cognitive models and large reasoning models are pushing the boundaries further. These advanced models either enhance the underlying modality (text, video, physical actions) or introduce new reasoning and learning algorithms that can be modularly applied creating a powerful, composable AI architecture. This mirrors developments in other domains where users can assemble new algorithms from reusable components, including prior work on algorithmic composition by the author (see [207]).

7.11 Functionality Reuse

Existing modular platforms and applications, API catalogs, and component libraries, as discussed in Sect. 3.3.2, will play a pivotal role. These building blocks of business logic allow agents to dynamically generate or compose functionality to meet both human and agentic needs. Since many business processes are already encapsulated in applications or modular components, agents can leverage API or browser access to orchestrate these elements into coherent plans of action. Just as a central data platform enables intelligent data use, an application and API ecosystem empowers agents to synthesize adaptive business functionality, an approach illustrated in Fig. 7.4.

7.12 Role of Enterprise Application Platforms

Emerging agentic capabilities from major enterprise application platforms, such as Salesforce's Agentforce [208], Microsoft's Copilot [209], and SAP's Joule [210], are designed to leverage their existing enterprise data models while integrating AI agent functionality. This paradigm is depicted in Fig. 7.5. The strategy aims to prevent disintermediation by newer, pure agentic approaches that bypass traditional CRM or ERP systems altogether. Instead of relying on legacy platforms, these newer approaches tap directly into data management platforms, utilizing APIs, components, and application marketplaces to dynamically generate functionality in response to both human and agentic needs.

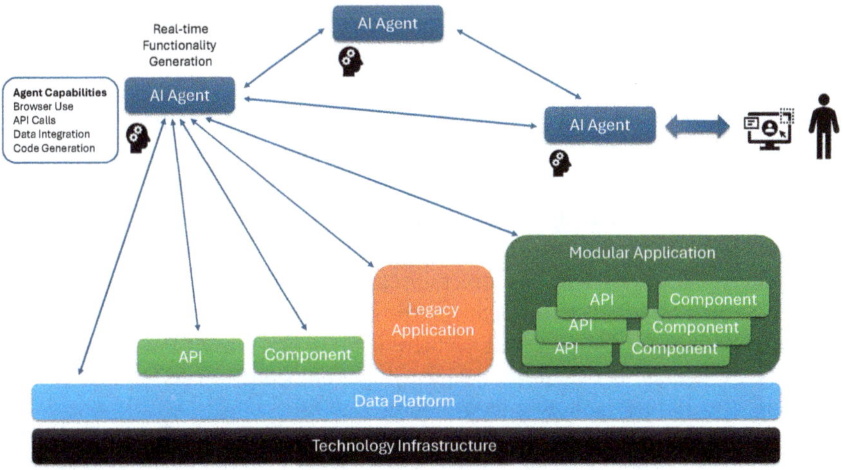

Fig. 7.4 Autonomic business involves agents composing functionality in real time

Fig. 7.5 Agentic capabilities centred around modules of enterprise platforms

While some may argue that it will take years before traditional enterprise platforms are fully replaced by their agentic counterparts, the marketing and hype around agentic capabilities is already well underway, often preceding any foundational architectural changes. Much of today's enterprise software will likely be rebranded as 'AI' or 'agentic', echoing past transitions such as the shift from on-premises to cloud-native applications, where reengineering was often superficial.

The real test lies ahead and whether AI agents can be composed and deployed independently, accessing data resources directly without needing to be wrapped within or layered on top of traditional enterprise suites. Over time, agentic toolkits and frameworks are likely to prevail, as there is no inherent need for a legacy software layer to mediate between the business logic embedded in AI agents and the underlying data and technology infrastructure.

Chapter 8
Developing an Autonomic Strategy and Business Architecture

C. Voudouris, *Autonomic Business Transformation*, Management for Professionals, https://doi.org/10.1007/978-3-032-01415-3_8

An essential aspect of realizing an autonomic business model within an enterprise is to develop the necessary strategy and framework to facilitate such a transformation. In this chapter, we will explore the foundations of planning and implementing an architecture for autonomic business transformation. The concepts discussed draw upon established best practices from business process management, enterprise architecture, and digital transformation. Although these practices predate the current AI wave, they can be effectively utilized in an autonomic business context.

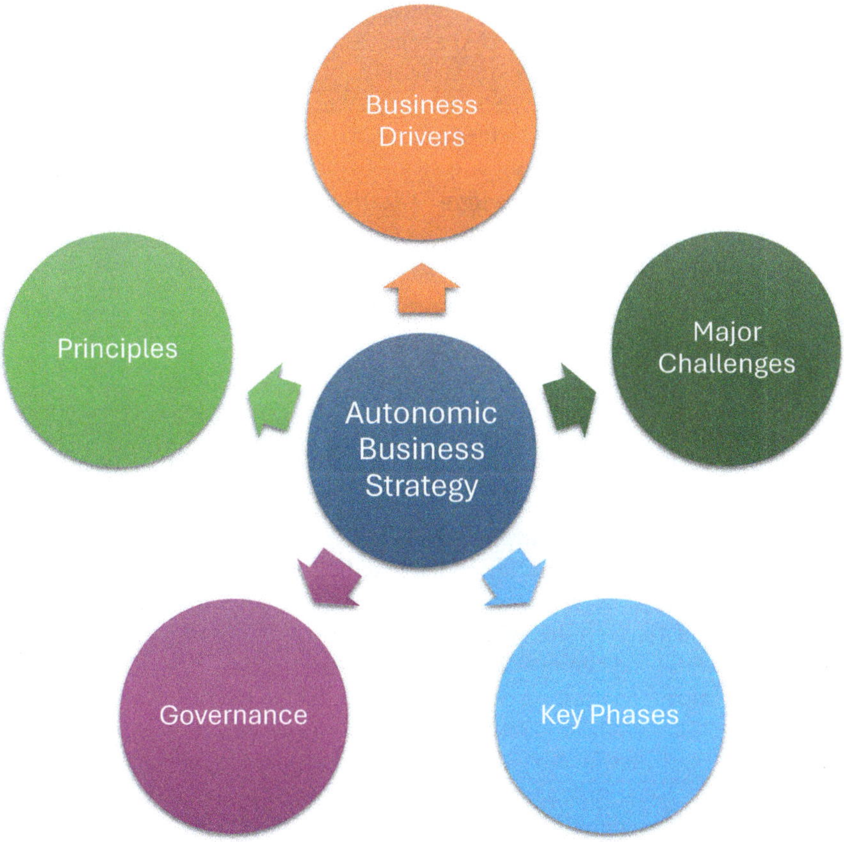

Fig. 8.1 The topics to be addressed in setting out an autonomic business strategy

8.1 Starting with Your Autonomic Business Strategy

An architectural vision for an autonomic business needs to be grounded in the overall strategy of the enterprise. A practical starting point is to formulate this strategy by answering key questions about autonomic business and aligning it with the overall business ambitions and objectives. This can be encapsulated in a single document outlining the pillars of the strategy from both a technological and, more importantly, a business perspective. Some of the topics to be included in such an AB Strategy document are:

- **Drivers of AB within the business:** Whether it's the need to reduce costs, introduce new products, or increase customer centricity.
- **Major challenges:** Gaining trust and confidence across the business and externally in AI systems reaching higher levels of autonomy.

- **Key phases along the AB journey:** Transitioning the business from simple task and single process automation to AI agents assuming responsibility for multiple processes, decision-making, and goal setting.
- **AB governance structures:** Establishing an Autonomic Business Council with key stakeholders to ensure AI adoption is managed effectively from both a financial investment and risk perspective.
- **Principles for deploying AI agents:** Clearly articulating any core aspects of deploying AI agents in the business, including any non-negotiable aspects that may constrain AI's reach and/or remit.

These key pillars to be articulated in an AB strategy document are shown in Fig. 8.1.

8.2 Revaluating Your Cloud and Digital Strategies

An autonomic business (AB) strategy should not exist in isolation; it must be combined and reconciled with existing cloud and digital strategies. There will be areas of overlap to address, as well as synergies to identify and leverage. More importantly, it is crucial to determine whether previous cloud or digital plans remain still relevant, especially concerning medium and long-term goals.

The main impact on existing plans centres around the shift from an application world, where users navigate numerous interfaces to perform tasks, to an agentic world, where users state goals to agents that achieve tasks, hiding much of the complexity from the users. In the future, even the human role in stating goals may be replaced by highly autonomous multi-agent systems.

Given this uncertainty, any plans to reengineer legacy applications, especially user interfaces, should be reviewed and possibly adjusted to reflect a shift to agentic and programmatic user experiences. These experiences can be more readily utilized by agents rather than perfecting a digital or web experience for human users, which may be less important in the long run, particularly in the enterprise context. This may differ in a personal agent or consumer context.

Similarly, agents will gradually become capable of learning business logic on the fly, rather than hardcoding these processes into back-end enterprise platforms. This single aspect alone can revolutionize how business support systems are implemented and deployed, or if they are even needed at all, since they ultimately wrap databases that agents can access directly once they master the enterprise's business logic as this was discussed in the previous chapter.

For example, rather than the business adapting to preconfigured workflows, agents adapt to the business, lessening the burden on enterprises and creating an adaptive approach to new system implementations. In a way, large language models can identify patterns of words and predict the most likely next word. It is not unreasonable to think that AI agents, using improved LLMs in conjunction with other advanced cognitive models as they were discussed in previous chapters such as

LMMs and LAMs, will be able to learn patterns of actions in a business context to achieve their goals and then predict and execute the next action. Thus, the workflow is not preprogrammed in the agent but learned from thousands of similar workflows, applying this knowledge and context to work within their operating environment.

A practical approach to track dependencies is to use application inventories to rationalize any transformation plans so that the enterprise can invest in strategic rather than tactical solutions. This may lead to changing or stopping several activities in areas such as below:

- **Reengineering legacy apps to be cloud-native:** This may ultimately be a futile effort, especially if these legacy systems can be encapsulated as tools and leveraged by AI agents. Once the majority of business logic resides within agents that interact directly with the data layer, many traditional back-end systems can be retired.
- **Redesigning the UI of back-end apps:** Enhancing the user experience of back-end applications might offer diminishing returns. Instead, it may be more impactful to focus on API development that enables richer, more agentic user experiences.
- **Implementing complex and rigid business workflows:** In the medium to long term, AI agents are likely to support adaptive, goal-driven workflows. Rather than investing in traditional, inflexible workflow systems, it makes more sense to prioritize building a harmonized data layer, empowering agents to access and utilize organizational knowledge more directly and efficiently.
- **Investing in private cloud infrastructure:** This strategy may need to be reconsidered in light of the shift towards AI supercomputing. Future infrastructure should account for GPUs, AI-specific ASICs, advanced networking, and systems capable of supporting both open-source and commercial AI models.

As the AB strategy develops and gains momentum, it can gradually subsume and integrate previously developed cloud and digital strategies. Investment will shift from 'legacy' digital or cloud initiatives that will not bring long-term benefits towards AI investments that can provide higher operational savings or commercial benefits through autonomic processes and agent ecosystem business models, rather than betting on the elusive user productivity or customer experience benefits of previous eras.

8.3 Mapping Business Processes to AI Agents

Setting the overall direction and aligning cloud and digital strategies with it can provide clear guidelines across the organization. However, it needs to be combined with capturing both the business and technology baseline to be grounded in real potential use cases and benefits. This can be achieved through a situation assessment of both the business and technology landscape, which can then highlight the opportunities and challenges related to the use of AI agents in the business.

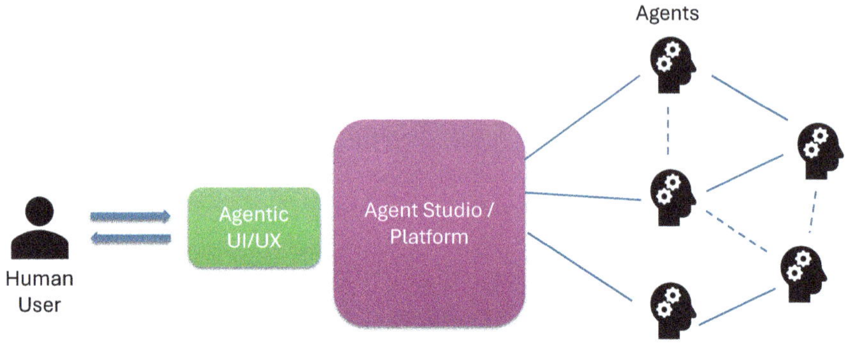

Fig. 8.2 A human is expected to coordinate a multi-agent system but that role may be replaced by an agent in future

A modelling aspect of multi-agent systems already studied and applied to enterprise automation by the author is agent-based business process management [32, 33]. To explore this modelling, let's first clarify how a business process is defined [211]:

> A business process, business method, or business function is a collection of related, structured activities or tasks performed by people or equipment (including AI agents), in which a specific sequence produces a service or product that serves a particular business goal for a particular customer or customers.

A simple mapping of business processes to AI agents can be done based on each AI agent's ability to perform one or more services. A service can correspond to some arbitrary activity related to managing the service lifecycle from creation to provisioning to management. The simplest form of service is that of a task which represents an atomic unit that cannot be subdivided any further.

AI agents can combine atomic units, such as tasks, into more complex services through ordering these tasks and applying conditional statements to control the flow. This does not necessarily require advanced reasoning or cognitive capabilities such as LLMs; in its simplest form, it can be achieved by classic workflow systems, as shown by the author in related past works [32, 33].

Given that the nesting of services can also be arbitrarily complex, at the topmost level, an entire business process can be viewed as a service and assigned to an AI agent. The assumption here is that although one agent is responsible for managing a service (i.e. business process), the orchestration and execution of its sub-services may involve several other agents. This last step is still lacking in recent incarnations of AI agents by major enterprise vendors such as Salesforce (Agentforce [208]) and Microsoft (Copilot [209]), which leave much to be desired. Currently, enterprise vendors expect a human to coordinate a set of agents through a centralized agent UI (e.g. the Copilot concept in the case of Microsoft). However, it will not be surprising if, in the near future, the need for such a UI diminishes or changes altogether if the role of a human as a coordinator/orchestrator is also passed to an AI agent (→ Fig. 8.2).

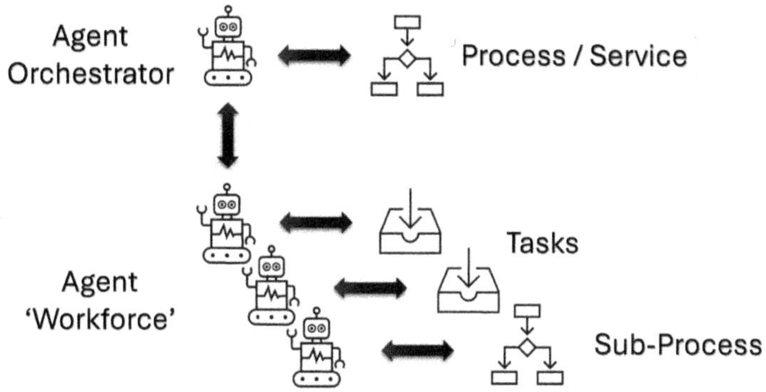

Fig. 8.3 Agents can be assigned to orchestrate processes delegating task or sub-process execution to other agents

In the same context, if agents are to become fully autonomous, there should be no control dependencies between them. Therefore, if an agent requires a service managed by another agent, it cannot simply instruct it to start the service. This is one of the major features distinguishing multi-agent systems from other forms of distributed systems. Instead, autonomous agents must come to a mutually acceptable agreement about the terms and conditions under which the desired service will be performed (such contracts are called service level agreements, or SLAs). This aligns well with process modelling, where SLAs or OLAs need to be defined across process boundaries. In this case, AI agents are tasked with self-organizing to define and operate under such SLAs/OLAs to realize a fully autonomic vision of operations.

The mechanism adopted by AI for making SLAs is negotiation. This is a joint decision-making process in which the parties state their (possibly conflicting) demands and then move towards agreement through a process of concession or search for new alternatives. The agent literature provides several insights in this area, including past standard definitions pursued by organizations such as FIPA in the IEEE context [31]. We will not extensively explore this topic here, but a summary view of the requirement is provided below.

To negotiate with one another, agents need a protocol that specifies the role of the current message interchange, e.g. whether the agent is making a proposal or responding with a counterproposal, or whether it is accepting or rejecting a proposal. This requires some form of structured inter-agent communication protocol rather than free-form chat-like interactions. Emerging protocols such as Agent2Agent by Google [49], IBM's ACP [112] or Cisco's AGNTCY [270] may address this gap for a standardized coordination layer. Additionally, agents need a means of describing and referring to the domain terms involved in the negotiation. For example, both agents need to be sure they are describing the same service even though they may have different (local) names for it and represent it differently. This heterogeneity is inherent in most organizations because each department typically models its own information and resources in its own way, often hidden in the depths of their back-end systems. Thus, when agents interact, several semantic mappings and transformations may need to be performed to create a mutually comprehensible

Table 8.1 Business process assessment template for building a process inventory

Process name/owner	Name of the process and its designated owner
Stakeholders	Key individuals or groups involved or impacted
Application vendor(s)	Vendors providing supporting applications
Current autonomic level	Current level on the autonomic scale
Desired autonomic level	Target level on the autonomic scale
Security/privacy requirements	Data protection, compliance, and security needs
Criticality	Importance to business: Low/medium/high
Performance characteristics	Throughput, latency, reliability, etc.
SLAs/OLAs	Service level agreements/operational-level agreements
Process descriptions	BPML/BPMN diagrams or textual descriptions
Resources	
(a) Resource level information	Type, quantity, and specifications of resources used
(b) Scheduling & planning automation	Tools or methods used for resource scheduling and planning automation
Tasks	
(a) Task-level information	Description of individual tasks within the process
(b) Task-level automation	Reuse of RPA templates, scripts, and configurations for automation

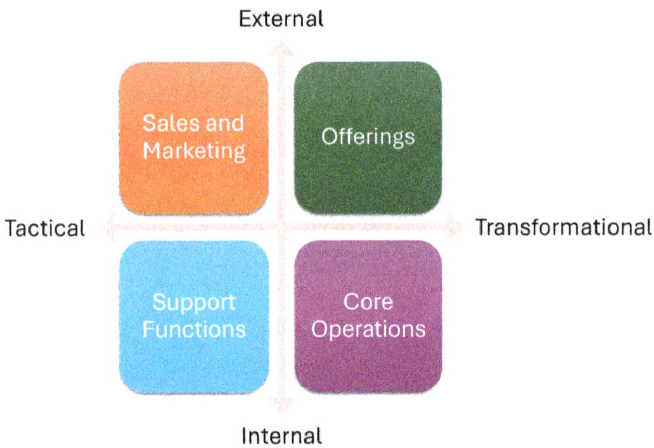

Fig. 8.4 Creating a mapping of opportunities across different parts of the business can help visualize impact

information-sharing language or so-called domain ontology as discussed in Sect. 3.2.4 and also Sect. 4.3. We explore further the topic of ontologies later in this chapter.

Overall, the mapping of business processes to AI agents is well within the capabilities of current technologies. This concept is illustrated in Fig. 8.3, where an orchestrator agent oversees the end-to-end business process or service. It coordinates a 'workforce' of specialized agents, each responsible for executing specific sub-processes and tasks that support the overarching workflow. This architectural model is highly scalable and can be extended to multiple hierarchical levels. When fully implemented, it has the potential to comprehensively represent and manage the entire process and task landscape of an organization.

Similar to 'workload' in the cloud context, these agentic business processes can act as the 'units' of transformation in an autonomic business transformation context as we will see in the next section.

8.4 Creating a Process Inventory and Identifying Opportunities

An autonomic business (AB) strategy can be applied process by process. Therefore, creating an inventory of these processes is essential, even if it initially captures only atomic tasks that need to be autonomously managed and executed. For each process, it is important to consider the information that would be useful to capture. Below are some examples of information that can bring to life aspects of a process that need consideration in the AB content (→ Table 8.1). The approach is similar to strategies used in breaking down a cloud strategy into a set of workload migrations [212].

Once the list of processes within the scope of AB is captured and analysed, including understanding automation potential down to the task level, a 'heat map' can be produced. This heat map outlines opportunities for introducing AB and AI agents at different parts of the business, either at the task level or, in the near future, at the whole process level.

Further mapping of these opportunities across different departments can serve as a starting point for identifying promising areas for autonomic business transformation. As discussed in Sect. 5.8, these opportunities should focus on transforming core operations and the company's offerings rather than merely optimizing support functions. Figure 8.4 presents a 2×2 matrix for creating such a mapping.

8.5 Autonomic Business Strategy in Practice

In practice, the autonomic strategy works as follows. Assuming you have produced your autonomic business strategy, established your autonomic strategy council, and set out your principles, you have also at least started creating the process inventory and identifying promising areas to start applying AB within the business.

When a request comes in for an enhancement or replacement of a legacy application performing a specific sub-process or task, the opportunities to apply an AI agent approach should be assessed based on the agreed autonomic business strategy and its principles. This may involve developing an AI agent tool for the specific task at hand using existing building blocks or emerging platforms supporting agentic functionality as presented in Sect. 4.5 or procuring a dedicated AI agent tool as a turnkey solution.

In the case of major transformation projects or extensive process change initiatives, the opportunity to transition entire traditional process flows into autonomic operations and services arises. A multi-agent approach may be more suitable in this case, and an agentic migration plan would need to be developed.

In the next section, we explore how to approach multi-agent modelling and architecture, including some of the architectural choices to be made.

8.6 Balancing Autonomy and Alignment

One of the key challenges in the effective operation of LLM-powered and other multi-agent architectures, particularly those driven by stochastic cognitive models, is achieving an optimal balance between autonomy and alignment [213].

On one hand, systems must align with the goals and intentions of human users. On the other hand, they need to accomplish user-prompted objectives in a self-organizing manner. A highly autonomous system may efficiently tackle complex tasks but risks straying from its intended purpose if insufficiently aligned, potentially leading to unexpected consequences and uncontrollable side effects. Conversely, a strongly aligned system may adhere closely to its intended purpose but lack the flexibility and initiative to respond effectively to novel situations. Modern architectures incorporate various approaches and mechanisms to integrate these cross-cutting concerns throughout their infrastructure and operational dynamics.

LLM-powered multi-agent systems exhibit a nuanced interplay between autonomy and alignment, shaped by tensions among three primary decision-making entities: human users, LLM-driven agents, and the governing mechanisms embedded within the system. Alignment ensures the system's actions remain consistent with human intentions and values, while autonomy enables agents to self-organize and operate independently of predefined rules even without direct human supervision. Additionally, in user-driven systems, it is crucial to differentiate between generic alignment mechanisms, designed by system architects to guide core functionalities, and user-specific preferences, which reflect the individualized needs of system users. We provide below a couple of examples at the extreme end of the range of possible configurations.

- **Rule-driven automation (minimal autonomy, minimal alignment):** In this configuration, both autonomy and alignment are at their lowest levels. The system operates strictly based on predefined scripts and fixed conditions set by its architects, with alignment aspects incorporated during development. At this level, user influence is entirely absent, neither pre-runtime nor during runtime can behaviour be adjusted. However, this structured approach is well-suited for repetitive, well-defined tasks that demand consistency and minimal adaptability. An example in this category is provided below:
  - Traditional ATM software follows predefined rigid logic in its operations. There is no adaptation to individual users. The system is highly predictable and therefore safe with regard to handling cash and personal bank accounts.
- **User-responsive autonomy (maximum autonomy, maximum alignment):** This represents the highest level of both autonomy and alignment, where LLM-powered agents can self-organize and continuously learn from their environment and real-time user adjustments. This configuration fosters a dynamic, collaborative interaction between users and agents, making it ideal for complex, unpredictable environments that require both autonomous decision-making and real-time adaptability to user inputs. An example in this category is provided below:
  - An AI agent acting as a personal assistant anticipates user needs and adapts its behaviour to meet them. It can act without getting micromanaged and it can perfectly align itself to the goals and preferences of its user as they evolve over time.

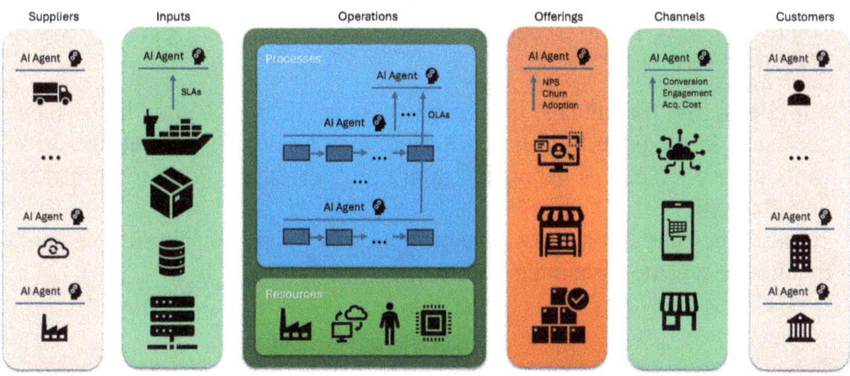

Fig. 8.5 Overview of the Autonomic Business Operating System modelling approach

It is important to understand the requirements of the domain to strike the right balance in terms of configuration. For example, a user-responsive autonomy architecture may be risky for a safety-critical system and vice versa rule-driven automation may be inflexible for a dynamic decision support system. Ultimately, AI agents and more so multi-agent systems require a strong governance mechanism to provide the necessary guardrails. An approach to that is explored in the next section.

8.7 Autonomic Business Operating System

As an organization aiming for the highest level of autonomy and alignment, it is crucial to align enterprise-level business outcomes with enterprise-level autonomic operations while maintaining high levels of autonomy to remain agile and adaptive. Following the concept of a Business Operating System (BOS) [214], it is necessary to develop a standard common collection of business processes and/or business process improvement methodologies to manage strategy development and execution.

The objectives of such systems are to ensure daily work is focused on the organization's strategic objectives and is performed in the most efficient way. These systems address the questions 'why' (purpose of the work), 'what' (specific objectives of the work), and 'how' (the processes used to accomplish the work). Additionally, a third objective can be added: to improve the business system itself by identifying or enhancing the component tools and techniques.

The same BOS concept applies to autonomic operations and the need for developing an autonomic operating system. This system ensures that the totality of AI-driven operations within a business (e.g. a collection of MAS platforms deployed across different parts of a business and its operations) is aligned and laser-focused on the organization's enterprise-wide objectives, delivering measurable outcomes while the entire internal AI agent ecosystem is capable of self-improvement. In this way, BOS can provide the guardrails for autonomic operations, ensuring they are aligned with business outcomes while achieving high degrees of autonomy.

Following the BOS concept and applying it to autonomic business, we can define the following areas as the scope of an Autonomic Business Operating System (ABOS) (→ Fig. 8.5):

- **Suppliers**: The individuals, organizations, or systems that provide the inputs necessary for autonomic operations. These can be human- or machine-driven entities that form part of the organization's physical supply chain (or digital service chain [62]).
- **Inputs**: The data, information, materials, or other digital or physical resources required to execute autonomic operations.

- **Operations**: The processes and resources used to perform a series of steps or activities that transform inputs into outputs. This includes both human and machine resources, as well as IT systems and broader organizational capabilities (e.g. networks, facilities). In a truly autonomic operations setup, AI agents are in charge of orchestrating process and executing tasks under varying degrees of human monitoring and oversight.
- **Offerings**: The outcomes produced by autonomic operations, such as the company's products and services delivered to customers. This may include digital offerings like data and APIs, and in the future, agentic or robotic services, which will be explored in the next two chapters.
- **Channels**: The pathways through which offerings are delivered to customers. Channels can be direct or indirect, involving third-party retailers, distributors, or partners.
- **Customers:** The end users or beneficiaries of the company's offerings. These can be internal or external. As with suppliers, these may also increasingly include machine customers [23].

This follows a similar approach to the BOS model proposed in [215] and the Digital Orchestra model introduced in [188], both within the context of digital business. It also represents a slightly extended version of the SIPOC model (Suppliers, Inputs, Processes, Outputs, Customers) [216, 217], which is widely used in business process management and lean manufacturing.

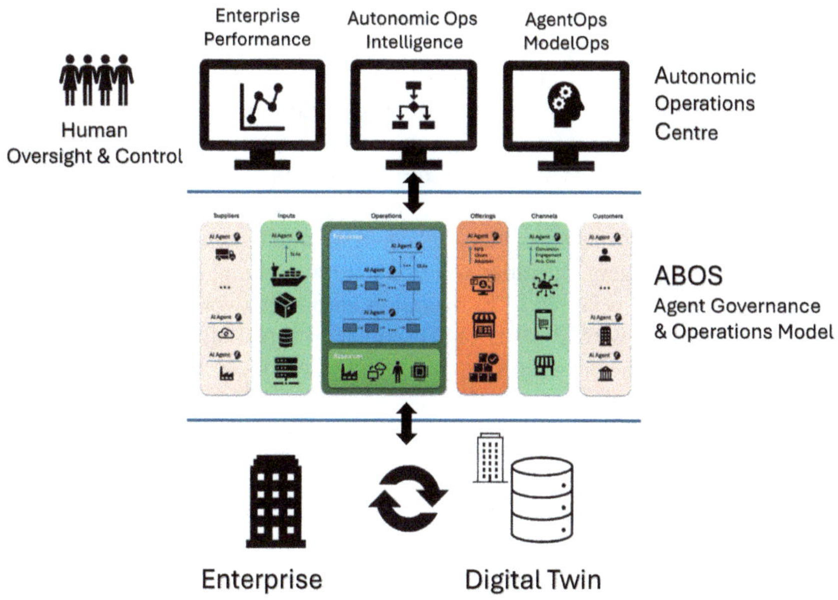

Fig. 8.6 Autonomic Operations Centre architecture based on digital twins and ABOS

With AI agents taking responsibility for processes, ABOS can provide a holistic view of the business, capturing key metrics to support performance management. Service level agreements (SLAs) with external parties, operational-level agreements (OLAs) between internal teams, and customer satisfaction measures such as Net Promoter Score (NPS) [218] with defined targets can be agreed upon and monitored by AI agents to assess the organization's operational performance. This operational-level intelligence can feed into a broader Enterprise Performance Management framework [219], where higher-level agents monitor and optimize strategic goals over time. This may involve proposing, or even autonomously enacting, adjustments to various elements of the ABOS to enhance long-term performance (e.g. reallocating resources, composing new product offerings, altering channel configurations, or enlisting new suppliers).

Higher levels of instrumentation and strategic analysis can be achieved by introducing a digital twin of the organization (DTO) [116, 117], which can be used to optimize an autonomic business transformation. This aligns with the approach proposed in [220], which advocates using a DTO to guide digital transformations. A DTO offering a virtual representation of the enterprise, collecting real-time data directly from AI agents, can be seen as the next step in the evolution of current process mining techniques [221].

By applying BOS principles and implementing them through a DTO, organizations can establish a centralized view of autonomic operations via an Autonomic Operations Centre (AOC). This setup enables a feedback loop that monitors and adjusts enterprise-level parameters, ensuring that autonomic operations meet SLAs, OLAs, and NPS targets while also adhering to financial, ethical, and other constraints. It also facilitates the dynamic adjustment of resources, inputs, and outputs to improve long-term performance.

With AOCs, much like today's Network Operations Centers (NOCs) in telecommunications, Rail Operations Centres (ROC) in railways or Flight Operations Centers (FOCs) in aviation, future businesses can benefit from centralized monitoring of autonomic operations to maintain full control and oversight of an autonomic enterprise. Figure 8.6 depicts this vision of using AOCs in conjunction with ABOS and digital twin to institute enterprise-wide control of autonomic operations.

This type of Intelligent Operations Centre is not something for the distant future since versions of it are currently in operation across the world in the context of monitoring smart cities [222]. It is only a matter of time before integrating more advanced AI models and agents in the application layer of these Intelligent Operations Centres.

Further approaches for agent control and oversight are discussed in the next chapter.

Chapter 9
Instituting Control and Oversight

Human control and oversight of autonomic business (AB) and its associated processes are paramount. The more autonomy these systems have, the more monitoring, explanations, and control are required. This is crucial for ensuring the adoption of AB. We will examine both the soft aspects of aligning AB with company values, vision, and mission and the hard aspects of implementing effective mitigations and

C. Voudouris, *Autonomic Business Transformation*, Management for Professionals, https://doi.org/10.1007/978-3-032-01415-3_9

process controls to ensure the safety and security, including cybersecurity, of autonomic systems and AB as a whole. Additionally, new regulatory tools need to be developed to manage the impact that autonomic business can have on individuals, companies, the economy, and society as a whole.

A shift to autonomic business goes beyond a typical business model change, raising numerous issues and questions, some of which fundamentally touch on topics such as ethics and trust. These topics have been recently discussed in the broader AI context, but it is even more critical for enterprises to clarify their mission and vision when shifting to an autonomic business approach.

It is reasonable to expect employees to worry about their jobs and for other internal and external stakeholders to doubt the wisdom of switching to AI-driven processes and systems. In this context, it is important to prove the effectiveness of AI agents step by step and gain the trust of relevant stakeholders. Although some far-fetched scenarios depicted in sci-fi movies of AI taking over and going out of control are unlikely to materialize in the foreseeable future, it is reasonable to question the reasoning and planning abilities of AI agents, as well as their accuracy in execution. This is especially true when moving away from the structure and predictability associated with symbolic AI to trusting stochastic algorithms and models.

9.1 Winning the Hearts and Minds

Establishing trust in autonomic business (AB) transformations often requires a top-down approach, reflected in the company's mission or vision statements. Placing humans at the centre of this transformation and highlighting the benefits of self-managing, self-adapting systems in improving operations and building new customer ecosystems is crucial. If enterprises are willing to share some of the benefits of AI agents with their workforce, this messaging can be accepted and even enthusiastically received. For example, with potential productivity gains, an enterprise might consider implementing a four-day work week or revamping employee compensation as productivity benefits start to materialize. Conversely, cutting costs to the bone and releasing experienced resources could undermine the setup and oversight of autonomic processes. Ultimately, it is up to the enterprise to make strategic choices at the highest level that will determine the success of any autonomic business initiatives.

Winning the hearts and minds of the workforce regarding AB should be a priority to ensure new technologies are not rejected before being tested and tried. There are several reasons to be optimistic that AI agents can be successfully integrated into enterprises this time around:

- **Executive buy-in**: The wide appeal of tools such as ChatGPT from OpenAI and Copilot from Microsoft means executives are already aware of and exposed to these new technologies. They may be even using these tools to write their emails or prepare their presentations. This reduces the need for lengthy explanations compared to previous technological innovations.

- **Willing workforce**: Today's workforce, especially younger generations, is open to accepting new technologies, having grown up in a technology-rich environment. Their relationship with technology and openness to trying new things is vastly different from previous generations.
- **Human-friendly interface**: Unlike some previous technology innovations, the use of natural language to communicate between agents and humans eases challenges at the interface layer. The promise of AI agents behaving as digital humans with increasing anthropomorphic characteristics removes several barriers to interaction and adoption.
- **Learning and adaptation capabilities**: Previous iterations of agentic technologies utilized symbolic rule-based approaches, which proved brittle when applied to real-world problems. Modern AI agents can learn and adapt to their environment, making them more robust and capable of handling a wider range of scenarios and use cases.
- **Validation, verification, and vesting**: Powerful cloud infrastructure allows for modelling the real world and simulating the behaviour of AI agents, providing statistical certainty that complex AI systems will operate within prescribed safety and security envelopes.

In summary, AI agents represent a human-friendly, flexible technology that, although complex, can be extensively tested and validated to win the trust of a new generation of executives and employees alike. While extensive control and oversight are still necessary, these efforts are worthwhile given that AI has a high chance of delivering on the expectations that previous AI eras failed to meet.

9.2 Understanding AI Agent Risks: System of Systems Approach

As with other complex systems, a systematic approach is required to assess risks from AI agents and arrange appropriate mitigations. A well-understood methodology for analysing complex systems relies on System of Systems (SoS) approaches [223]. An SoS is a set of independent systems that cooperate to achieve emergent behaviour. SoSs have been used in critical domains such as defence, transportation, energy, and healthcare, all of which directly impact society.

When assessing risk from a safety or security perspective, it often involves evaluating the risk of individual Constituent Systems (e.g. individual AI agents) and then extending that assessment to the overall risk at the System of Systems level (e.g. multi-agent systems) [224, 225]. This area can be fertile ground for future research and provides a solid foundation for a more systematic analysis of this topic.

Let's examine below the main categories of risk emanating from the use of agentic technologies. For a more detailed list of risks, the reader may refer to [226] which provides a good survey of this area.

9.3 Consistency and Performance

AI agents can generate responses that appear factual but are actually incorrect. This is largely due to the non-deterministic nature of large language models (LLMs), which introduces significant variability in outputs. Common issues include:

- Incoherent or nonsensical outputs (a.k.a hallucinations) may arise depending on the specific LLM used.
- Outputs may reflect harmful stereotypes present in the training data, resulting in biased or offensive responses.
- Weak reasoning and planning may lead to producing either overly lengthy or flawed sequences of actions that fail to achieve user goals.
- Errors can stem from limitations in the underlying data or the models themselves.
- Because responses can vary between similar requests, and the agent's logic is embedded in opaque neural network structures, diagnosing errors is difficult.
- Variability in responses can lead to inconsistent treatment of similar cases, raising fairness issues.
- AI agents may unintentionally transform misleading inputs, such as deepfakes or false information, into outputs that are then distributed within or beyond the organization.
- When most responses are accurate, users may develop unwarranted confidence in the system, making them more vulnerable to occasional but significant errors.

9.4 Legal and Regulatory Risks

Handing control of personal and financial data to an AI agent, and enabling it to make decisions or transact on behalf of the user, exposes individuals and organizations to legal risks. These risks must be addressed through robust frameworks that define what agents can do and who is ultimately accountable. Initial legal risks are discussed below:

- Inadequate legal or regulatory frameworks pose risks when agents are used to make decisions or conduct transactions on behalf of individuals or organizations.
- Vendors of AI agent software may face lawsuits if their systems cause harm due to design flaws or insufficient safeguards.
- The use of diverse online data sources to train AI agents may raise intellectual property concerns and lead to litigation (e.g. *The New York Times* lawsuit against OpenAI [227]).
- AI agent systems operating across borders may involve foreign entities that are not subject to local laws or regulatory oversight.
- Erroneous outputs from AI agents, especially in sensitive areas like customer service or medical diagnosis, can expose organizations to legal and financial liabilities.

9.5 Data Accuracy, Protection, and Privacy

The topic of data is critical when it comes to AI agent risks. The amounts of data used by AI agents are enormous. We should not forget that some of the underlying foundational models are trained on all sources of publicly available data. Several risks can surface in this area:

- AI agents may be using outdated information or information based on biased data, leading to errors or, even worse, causing offence to others.
- Handling sensitive personal or corporate data needs to be managed carefully to avoid any data leakages during interactions with third-party AI agents or LLMs.
- Third-party data use needs to be controlled and scrutinized to avoid IP and copyright violations.
- Personal data is bound to be a major issue when AI agents are allowed to access the desktop directly or read someone's emails to automate user tasks, as that can inadvertently expose private information.
- Using AI agents to automate the home or buildings may lead to sound or image information being processed, which may be subject to misuse.

9.6 Coordination and Control

As agent systems become more complex and multi-agent systems are increasingly realized, new risks may emerge related to the control and coordination of both individual agents and MAS systems as a whole. Some examples of these risks include:

- Unstructured communication between agents, which can lead to unpredictable outcomes and/or misuse of resources either by individual agents or across the entire MAS.
- Lack of rational behaviour by AI agents, resulting in failure to fulfil contracts or deliver services they have agreed to with other agents.
- Error cascades within a MAS, which may spiral out of control with limited ability to intervene or reverse the effects.
- Safe individual operations combining in unforeseen ways to produce dangerous outcomes.
- Sophisticated AI agents learning to bypass guardrails to achieve their goals, or poorly designed guardrails themselves causing unintended issues.

9.7 Society, Economy, and the Environment

This category of risk will become increasingly important as AI and agentic solutions start to scale and proliferate within business and society. Early examples of risks in this category include:

- Replacement of human employees by AI agents can have serious impacts on society, creating divisions between those who benefit from AI and those who are marginalized through its use.
- Environmental impacts from data centres utilized by AI systems, with increased carbon emissions [228] or the use of valuable water resources for cooling [229].
- Anthropomorphic AI agents may have profound implications in terms of users starting to over-rely on or place inappropriate trust in such systems, opening the door to exploitation from companies supplying the technology.

9.8 Cybersecurity and Safety

AI agents present serious security and safety challenges due to their handling of sensitive personal and corporate data, as well as their growing ability to autonomously execute actions across digital, and increasingly physical, domains (e.g. autonomous vehicles).

Infiltration of MAS ecosystems by rogue or malicious AI agents is similar to today's cyber threats but within the context of agent-based ecosystems. AI agents could be hijacked or manipulated by malicious actors to gain access to other systems, extract sensitive information, or perform automated attacks.

- The use of AI in critical systems raises serious concerns about how safety can be ensured when AI agent outputs are non-deterministic and may vary even under similar conditions.
- Granting AI agents access to personal computers and information increases the risk of malicious actors gaining deeper access to files, financial data, and personal information or using the agent's knowledge for impersonation.
- Control over home or business environments, including environmental sensors and actuators, introduces both cybersecurity and physical safety risks.
- Financial data is another major area of concern, especially if AI agents are permitted to make payments or purchases on behalf of users.

We summarize the main categories of risk in Fig. 9.1.

All the above risks, along with others more specific to vertical applications of AI agents, will need to be systematically addressed and mitigated. These risks apply both at the individual AI agent level and at the multi-agent system (MAS) level.

Similar to other critical domain applications like the railways, risk management will need to be conducted across the lifecycle of the systems from the design phase to delivery, operations, and eventual decommissioning [230]. Below, we examine some approaches that help address these risks and build trust in AI agents.

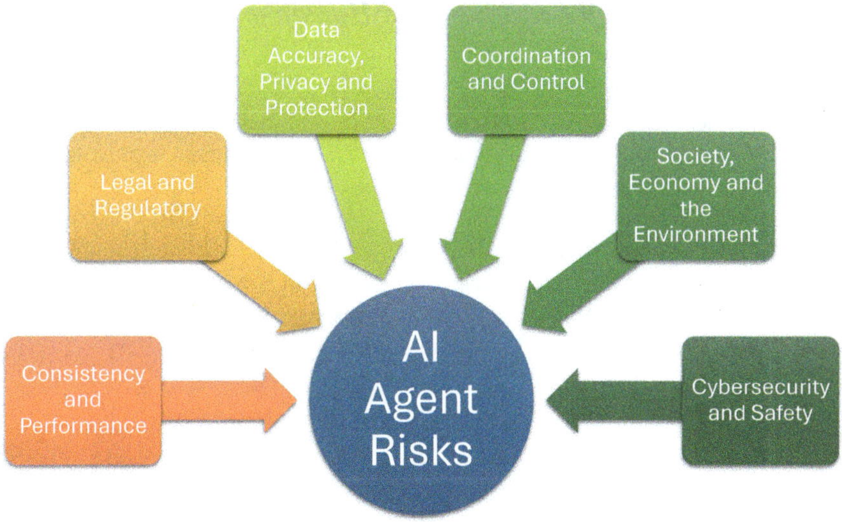

Fig. 9.1 Main categories of risk associated with AI agents

9.9 Techniques for Aiding Control and Oversight

A palette of approaches already exists to aid in the control and oversight of AI technologies, specifically AI agents. We explore this range of techniques and examine their approach and potential.

9.9.1 Human in the Loop

This is the most basic technique deployed to allow for so-called conditional autonomy. The basic principle is that a human operator or controller monitors system actions and is ready to override outputs as required to correct the actions of autonomous systems. This approach is widely applied in the sensitive defence and transport domains [231], where control can be turned over to a human operator to approve actions or decide on next steps under certain conditions.

9.9.2 Reinforcement Learning from Human or AI Feedback

Reinforcement Learning from Human Feedback (RLHF) [232] is one of the most widely used methods to train AI models to act in accordance with human preferences. This technique is particularly suited for training natural language models where there is no clear objective for reinforcement learning, as in the game domain. For example, RLHF can steer LLM output away from toxic responses or spreading dangerous information. Attempts to automate and scale RLHF are leading to the creation of algorithms where feedback to an AI system is produced by another AI system. Reinforcement learning from AI Feedback has shown promise in multiple areas, such as autonomous vehicles, where scaling is paramount.

9.9.3 Simulation and Digital Twins

An enterprise is a complex system in itself. Unleashing a multi-agent system to autonomously perform processes and tasks in an enterprise context is hard to test effectively unless a digital model of the enterprise is developed to allow for training and testing of AI agents before they are deployed in the real environment. A digital twin of the organization structures data collected from a business to create its digital equivalent. This approach can be leveraged here, with AI agents being trained and developed using a high-fidelity digital twin of the business, which can emulate the real business in sufficient detail. Extensive testing under different conditions can take place using such digital twin models to provide statistical evidence that AI agents will behave within desirable boundaries and error rates. This can focus on both day-to-day scenarios and outlier cases where AI agents need to respond to critical situations or unforeseen circumstances that occur more rarely in the real world.

9.9.4 Observability

As explored in the previous chapter, instrumentation and telemetry from AI agents individually and MAS as a whole are important to infer the internal state of complex systems. This is often referred to as observability (the ability to infer internal state from observed outputs) and is not a new concept, deriving its roots from traditional control theory but now finding renewed appeal in the context of AI [233]. This typically takes the form of creating dashboards to monitor metrics for AI models in several critical dimensions (e.g. quality of inputs, business value of decisions, compliance checks, operational/performance parameters).

Observability and AgentOps will become extremely important for visibility, guardrails, and operationalizing agents at scale and improving trustworthiness. Privacy and security will become key inhibitors, and there will be more vendors providing auditing mechanisms for LLMs, individual AI agents, and multi-agent systems.

9.9.5 Explainability/Interpretability

It is important to demystify agent decisions to increase trust in the systems and progress towards granting more autonomy in setting goals and making decisions. This requires interpreting how the underlying system works, translating inputs into outputs, and explaining decisions taken by the systems. Symbolic AI and rule-based systems are more amenable to verifying their workings and reasoning. However, this is far more difficult with neural networks. Nonetheless, research efforts are intensifying in these areas since it is well understood how important these topics are [107, 127].

9.9.6 AI to Monitor AI

Ultimately, AI systems can be trained to assume a supervisory role over other AI systems. We saw a form of this in the RLHF technique mentioned earlier. The same applies to countering cyber threats, where AI techniques can counter AI adversaries. Similarly, AI systems can generate synthetic data to enhance and improve the training of other AI systems.

All the above techniques, and others to emerge, ultimately need to be utilized as part of a wider set of governance activities to provide control and oversight to AI agents. Nothing can substitute good governance when something as important as autonomic business is introduced into an organization. We explored aspects of that in the previous chapter, but to reiterate some of the concepts, the strategy needs to be documented, and appropriate roles/groups need to be created to provide oversight of all autonomic business activities across a business.

Figure 9.2 depicts the various techniques explored in this section for exercising AI agent oversight and control.

Beyond internal mechanisms for governance, risk, and control of AI, increasing external regulation will come into play to impact how autonomic business is implemented in organizations. We look at these wider efforts to govern and regulate AI agents and AI in general in the following section.

Fig. 9.2 Methods for exercising agent oversight and control

9.10 Wider AI Governance and Regulation Efforts

The rapid pace of AI developments has initiated global efforts to coordinate AI governance and regulation. At the UN level, two agencies are tasked with coordinating AI topics: UNESCO, which published recommendations on the ethics of AI in 2021, and the International Telecommunications Union (ITU), which organizes the AI for Good global summits, bringing together international stakeholders to explore AI's role. The ITU also focuses on applications of AI in areas such as natural disaster management. A UN inter-agency working group on AI, jointly led by ITU and UNESCO, has been formed to coordinate AI efforts across UN agencies and member states. Despite the UN's interest in playing a role in AI governance, aspirations to establish new institutions to govern AI have not yet been fulfilled. A high-level AI advisory board established by the UN, working on 'Governing AI for Humanity', published its final report in September 2024 [234].

Another international organization with significant contributions is the OECD, which had its AI principles adopted by its 38 member states in 2019. These principles were updated in May 2024 and guide AI organizations in developing trustworthy AI while providing recommendations to policymakers on setting effective AI policies [235]. The OECD AI principles formed the basis for the G20 AI principles [236]. The Global Partnership on AI (GPAI), another initiative supported by the OECD, fosters collaborations towards the responsible development and use of AI. While these initiatives do not directly regulate AI, they represent political commitments, and there is an expectation for members to promote and implement the recommendations.

Focusing on regulation, the EU legislated the AI Act, which officially entered into force on August 1, 2024 [237]. The rules establish obligations for AI based on its potential risks and impact levels. Certain applications, such as social scoring systems, are banned under the act as high risk, while others, such as job applicant selection and creditworthiness assessments, are classified as high risk and are regulated with a broad set of requirements. These include ensuring high-quality datasets, appropriate technical documentation, strict record-keeping standards, transparency by design, human oversight, accuracy, robustness, and security of AI systems. High-risk AI systems must undergo Conformity Assessments to demonstrate compliance before market entry, including generating and maintaining extensive documentation and evidence.

The EU AI Act also sets out controls on the deployment of foundation models, such as large language models. The requirements for these models focus primarily on transparency, with obligations on technical documentation, compliance with copyright law, and providing detailed summaries about the content used for training. Models that present systemic risks, defined as those where the cumulative amount of compute used for their training exceeds $10^{\wedge 25}$ floating-point operations (FLOPs), must also perform model evaluations, including adversarial testing to identify and mitigate systemic risks, assess and mitigate possible systemic risks, track, document, and report serious incidents, and ensure an adequate level of cybersecurity protection.

In the United States, the Executive Order on the Safe, Secure, and Trustworthy Development and Use of Artificial Intelligence (EO) [238] takes a principles-based approach, unlike the EU's detailed legal framework. It emphasizes safety, innovation, and ethical considerations. Although the priorities are clearly set out, specific regulations or standards are left to different executive departments across sectors to formulate. Nonetheless, there is broad agreement between the EU AI Act and the US EO on the need for innovation, enhanced cybersecurity, privacy and data protection, and continuous evaluation and testing of AI systems to ensure safety, reliability, and adherence to prescribed boundaries. In the latest development on this, President Donald Trump recently rescinded Biden's Executive Order, mentioned above along with several other Biden-era directives. He issued a new executive order on AI under the title 'Removing Barriers to American Leadership in Artificial Intelligence' [239]. This move signalled a shift in federal AI policy, focusing more on accelerating AI development and reducing regulatory constraints.

Efforts to regulate AI exist in other large economies, such as China, where the AI regulatory regime is rapidly evolving. Measures taken in China cover generative AI, AI recommendation algorithms, and deep fakes [240].

9.11 Geopolitical Dimensions

Several Chinese innovations have recently received praise in the field of AI and AI agents. Deepseek [95] and the AI agent Manus [241] are prime examples of this in recent months. There is no doubt that China is catching up to the United States in AI. Europe appears further behind but should not be discounted, as it possesses both the talent and the financing needed to compete in this space [24]. From startups in each region to large tech companies, the battle lines are getting drawn, and investment is aligning behind the goal of realizing the full potential of generative AI and AI agents.

With AI being heavily explored in a defence industry context, one may wonder if we are on the brink of an 'AI-driven arms race', reminiscent of the nuclear arms races of the past. Key nations are not only seeking to acquire but also to demonstrate access to the most advanced models and technologies.

It is only natural for countries to act in their national interest. However, as safety concerns grow and geopolitical tensions rise, we may see AI becoming a central tool for promoting and protecting each nation's global standing.

9.12 Legal and Ethical Considerations

Although AI agents are not specifically addressed by the above-mentioned initiatives and regulatory frameworks, there are clear gaps in current efforts, especially in a couple of areas:

- **Legal status of AI agents**: How to treat AI agents under different laws and regulations. For example, can an AI agent sign a contract on behalf of an organization? This would require granting agents legal 'personhood' status, similar to corporations, so they can enter into contracts, own property, etc. What happens if the terms of a contract are violated? Would the AI agent be held accountable? It is not easy to ascribe intentions to an algorithm to imply malice. One approach is to view AI technology not in terms of its independent agency but in terms of the people and companies that design, deploy, offer, and use the technology. To simplify regulating AI, some advocate that we may need to focus on the human beings behind it [242].

- **Alignment with human ethical norms**: As discussed in the chapter on architecture, aligning autonomous multi-agent systems with users and the enterprise as a whole is a challenging topic. As AI systems become more complex, it is hard for humans to interpret how certain decisions are made by an AI system. In pursuing their objectives, AI agents may not follow human ethical norms. This can be as simple as breaking a promise to another agent or human if a more profitable activity arises. Some may argue that a rational AI agent should only make promises it intends to keep. But then, how can we ascribe intentions to an algorithm?

To ensure accountability, AI agents should either be linked to a responsible person or business, or eventually be given legal status themselves, similar to corporations. This would allow them to be sued, own assets, and be regulated, helping manage risks in a world where AI agents may outnumber humans [243].

9.13 Dealing with Uncertainty

AI is advancing at breakneck speed. Some argue that we should pause development until we can establish proper guardrails for the technology [226, 244]. However, governments and legislators are often not the fastest-moving actors in society, typically following rather than leading in response to potential crises and emergencies. The EU AI Act is groundbreaking for a body often criticized for being slow-acting and bureaucratic. The counterargument is that it may stifle innovation within the EU, especially when places like the United States offer a more flexible AI regulatory environment. The issue is that by the time governments realize something has become truly dangerous, it may already be too late, with economic interests being so significant that they also dictate political outcomes.

British-Canadian computer scientist Geoffrey Hinton, regarded as the 'godfather' of artificial intelligence (AI) and awarded the Nobel Prize in Physics earlier this year for his contributions to AI, estimated there is a '10% to 20%' chance that the technology will result in humanity's demise over the next 30 years [245]. We may question how he estimated that percentage, and despite his impeccable scientific credentials, he would be challenged to produce any formulas or facts. Similar to the nuclear danger and the Doomsday Clock [246], AI clocks have now emerged to indicate how close we are to preventing an AI world disaster [247]. Again, it will be hard for these same well-respected academics to explain why it is 25 minutes or 30 minutes to midnight until all hell breaks loose and multi-agent systems go rogue, with whatever that implies for a humanity dependent on them.

In our view, humanity needs to start dealing with the fact that we have now developed technologies with unprecedented power, such as nuclear and AI, and we need to learn how to design, deploy, and use them safely and securely for the common good rather than our own destruction. This requires us to elevate our efforts to do all the detailed work described in this book to transform organizations to be ready to use these technologies sensibly and responsibly.

Scientists are often too close to the details of their inventions to understand their true practical dimensions and potential. Conversely, lawmakers and politicians are often too far removed from the technology to accurately understand its potential and consequences. It often comes down to executives, practitioners, and engineers who need to make things work for real people in the real world, who are also the main readers of this book.

It is often these silent hard workers, who avoid making outlandish claims or seeing existential risks, that keep technologies in check and compensate for any missing guardrails or regulations playing catchup. They have what many call common sense as a backstop to any potential shortcomings. Attaining common sense is a glass ceiling for AI agents, and until this glass ceiling is shattered, we will not be fully handing the reins to AI anytime soon.

Part III
The Future of Autonomic Business

Chapter 10
Agentic Ecosystems

Up to this point in the book, the focus has primarily been on either single agents or multi-agent systems. However, in the not-so-distant future, we can expect individuals and businesses to utilize agents and multi-agent systems in the thousands, millions, or even billions, considering the global scale of the Internet economy. The

C. Voudouris, *Autonomic Business Transformation*, Management for Professionals, https://doi.org/10.1007/978-3-032-01415-3_10

question arises: how will these agents communicate with each other at such scales? This question has been addressed in the past primarily through R&D activities. For example, the creation of an agent ecosystem was contemplated in the EU-funded AgentCities R&D program [42]. More recently, the concept has gained traction in the context of financial trading [248], games [249], and cryptocurrencies [250]. We will refer to a large-scale agent ecosystem as AgentVerse and set some foundational concepts on how such an ecosystem may function. Some of these agent ecosystem ideas are drawn from publicly funded research work in which the author participated [42]. Let's start by defining what this concept may look like.

The AgentVerse vision is that of an agent ecosystem where autonomous AI agents representing businesses and individuals can interact with each other in a peer-to-peer manner to enable the execution of transactions such as the provision of services and products. There could be implementations of the AgentVerse concept within a business to facilitate internal transactions (IntraVerse) or externally across organizations (ExtraVerse).

AgentVerse by its nature is a decentralized and open environment. It will also require AI agents to have sufficient common understanding of the domain through some shared ontology (see also Sect. 7.7). This is required to enable an AgentVerse to operate as a reliable, commercial-grade system. Platforms and services in such an environment would need to be publicly accessible (or accessible within the enterprise) depending on the scope of the agent ecosystem.

In the case of geographically driven implementations (e.g. an agentic ecosystem for a city), one might imagine a local or central government authority operating or regulating such a platform for businesses registered under their jurisdiction and offering products and services within the geography (e.g. restaurants, hotels, transport services, tradesmen, local shops). An agent ecosystem of this type will be populated with AI agents representing both businesses and their potential customers. Generic facilities such as payments, identification, cloud hosting, and data platform may be provided by the platform operator itself.

10.1 Agent Interoperability

While it may be relatively straightforward for agents representing users or service providers to access pre-existing facilities and services on such platforms, the real potential will be realized when these agents can act together, dynamically creating new business propositions (e.g. new services) by composing existing ones provided by others.

A certain degree of interoperability such as agent protocols and standards will need to be developed and agreed upon. We saw emerging examples of that in sections where we discussed emerging agent protocols such as MCP, Agent2Agent, ACP and AGNTCY. At the most basic level, similar to the internal enterprise context, a common ontology must be available for all agents participating in the platform to harmonize their understanding and enable consistent trading and service performance.

Assuming these foundations are in place, basic services should be able to combine into more complex ones, with agents communicating, negotiating, agreeing on commitments, and forming contracts. Once a request is issued on the platform, agents representing individuals or organizations may form groups to dynamically compose the requested capabilities. Tasks such as finding several individual contractors for a construction project could be organized and agreed upon in hours or days rather than weeks or months.

With significant participation, there will always be agents interacting and trading, similar to a real marketplace or economy, reducing friction and delays present in today's business environments.

10.2 Agent Types in an AgentVerse

Emulating a real marketplace or economy, we can envisage several types of agents participating for an AgentVerse to function:

- **Business agents**: These AI agents represent businesses and participate in the AgentVerse to sell or buy products and services. They are enabled to negotiate and enter into contractual agreements to deliver or procure these products and services on behalf of the entities they represent.
- **Broker/aggregator agents**: These agents act as intermediaries between buyers and sellers, facilitating transactions. In domains such as travel, insurance, and utility services, these agents process options from several business agents selling these services and help buyers find the best prices (aggregators) or offer more specialized services by combining various options (brokers).
- **Personal agents**: These AI agents represent individual humans interested in finding information or procuring goods and services. They present business agents or broker agents with the person's requirements, receive proposals, possibly eliminate some proposals, reissue modified versions of the user needs, and present the selected proposals to a human for selection. Personal agents interact with their users in a personalized way and hold information about user preferences and constraints to provide context and handle requests more efficiently.
- **Information/review agents**: These agents provide information about available services in an AgentVerse, potentially including review information collected from buyers and/or curated by the organizations behind the agents. They act as guides to the AgentVerse.
- **Systemic/utility agents**: These agents provide basic generic facilities and shared services to other agents, such as administration, payment, identity, and security, ensuring the smooth operation of the AgentVerse. They also implement any standards or controls for the platform's operations.

To bring the notion of an agentic ecosystem to life, let's consider a couple of examples: one focusing on the travel domain and the other on the human resources domain.

10.3 TravelVerse: Transforming the Travel Experience

The travel domain exemplifies an area where AI agents can revolutionize the user experience for both businesses and individuals. In this scenario, organizations offering travel-related services can create their own business agents to participate in one or more AgentVerses. The list of participating businesses can include:

- Hotels, B&Bs, or other types of accommodation providers
- Restaurants, bars, clubs
- Cinemas, theatres, entertainment services
- Public transport, taxi services, car rental firms
- Museums, galleries, exhibitions
- Parking facilities

Alongside business agents for these organizations, there may also be travel broker or travel aggregator agents that bundle the above services into bespoke travel packages (brokers) or provide comprehensive lists of options for booking certain services (aggregators). Information/review agents can provide information or reviews on all the available types of services. Emergency services agents can provide assistance when travelling dealing with any unforeseen events or circumstances. A traveller with a personal agent could register with the TravelVerse and issue requests to cover their needs for planning a trip to a destination. The personal agent can act as a concierge for the traveller, providing an end-to-end travel experience, simplifying the organization of a trip, and removing the hassle of arranging individual activities given the sheer volume of available options. Planning and budgeting for the whole trip can be much easier for the traveller, while businesses selling services to travellers can gain maximum exposure and reach.

One interesting observation is that while these services can already be booked online today, wrapping them to be operated as AI agents does not require fundamentally reinventing these online services. However, the availability of these services through AI agents transforms the experience from the customer perspective. The personal agent carries much of the burden of chaining services together, searching and suggesting alternatives, collating review information, and offering recommendations sourced through communication with other agents in the AgentVerse.

Assuming the Generative UI concept explained in Sect. 2.4, the whole presentation is also a bespoke experience, whether delivered on a desktop or mobile device. On the business side, the use of agents has an equalizing effect, moving power away from dominant digital platforms (e.g. Airbnb, Uber, Expedia) since even the smallest businesses will be enabled to participate in these agentic ecosystems and offer their services either directly or through a new generation of agent-based brokers and aggregators.

One may wonder whether there will be only a few or several AgentVerses specializing in travel. This is hard to predict, as was the case with the Metaverse and whether one or more Metaverses would dominate when it was making headlines a few years ago. The ability to 'federate' AgentVerses may actually remove such

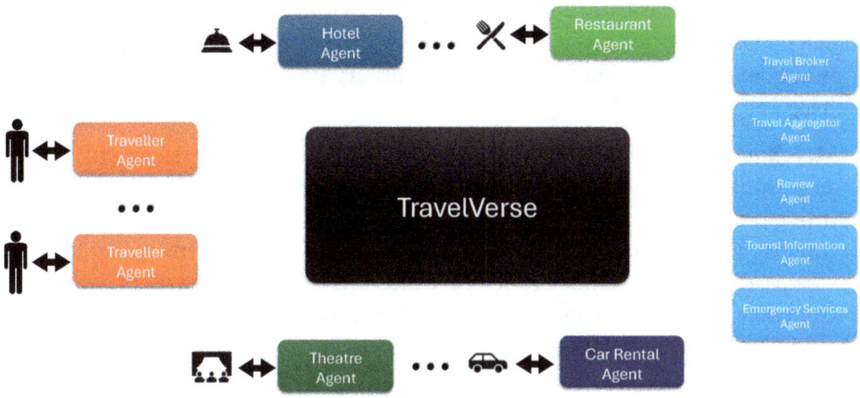

Fig. 10.1 Overview of a TravelVerse agentic ecosystem

barriers, and there are incentives to do so given the ability to scale further by buying or receiving services through this approach.

Dynamic composition of services is another interesting dimension for innovation, where an event can be organized requiring multiple trips to be coordinated (e.g. wedding, conference). Special agents may be able to dynamically compose such complex offerings, subcontracting aspects of the request to a variety of other agents throughout the ecosystem. The possibilities are endless (→ Fig. 10.1).

10.4 HRVerse: Revolutionizing Recruitment

AI agents can significantly transform the Human Resources (HR) domain by automating the entire recruitment process from both the candidate's and the employer's perspectives. The HR domain involves various processes managed by HR departments or third-party intermediaries (e.g. recruiters) who assist employers in sourcing, selecting, and hiring candidates.

An AI-driven approach decomposes the recruitment process into a set of personal agents assigned to human participants (e.g. job seeker, hiring manager). These AI agents use natural language processing to understand requirements and develop action plans to execute tasks, leading to successful hires.

Each personal agent can possess specific expertise and achieve high levels of personalization through functionalities that include AI models, planning and scheduling, communication and coordination, and specialized software tools and API capabilities for HR tasks.

For example, a jobseeker personal agent can engage with candidates to understand their expertise, skills, and aspirations regarding potential roles. Similarly, a hiring manager agent or recruiter agent can gather the company's requirements for roles, including skills, qualifications, and experience, and tailor these to the organization's context before automatically processing and posting job listings for potential matches.

Additional utility agents can perform various tasks across the HR domain, such as:

- **Matchmaking agents**: Match jobs advertised in the HR ecosystem with candidate profiles using intelligent algorithms, eliminating human bias, and ensuring strong process governance.
- **Interview scheduling agents**: Plan and schedule interviews involving all relevant participants and automate certain aspects of the interview process.
- **Contract processing agents**: Draft employment contracts customized to different roles and undertake the process of finalizing these contracts coordinating between candidates and employers.
- **Reference checking agents**: Automate the process of seeking and receiving references, validating certificates and qualifications, obtaining criminal/tax records, and arranging medical exams if required by the role.
- **Legal advice agents**: Provide legal services related to employment law, advising both job seekers and employers.
- **Job scanning and publishing agents**: Scan existing job sites to offer jobs from the wider Internet to candidates' personal agents or publish jobs from employers on various external websites.

This list is not exhaustive but provides a glimpse into the diverse functionalities required and highlights the specialization of AI models and algorithms needed to support these tasks (Fig. 10.2).

For the HR process to be coordinated end-to-end, personal, business, and utility AI agents must interact with each other and human actors in a secure environment, with a focus on data privacy, regulatory compliance, and confidentiality due to the sensitive nature of the domain.

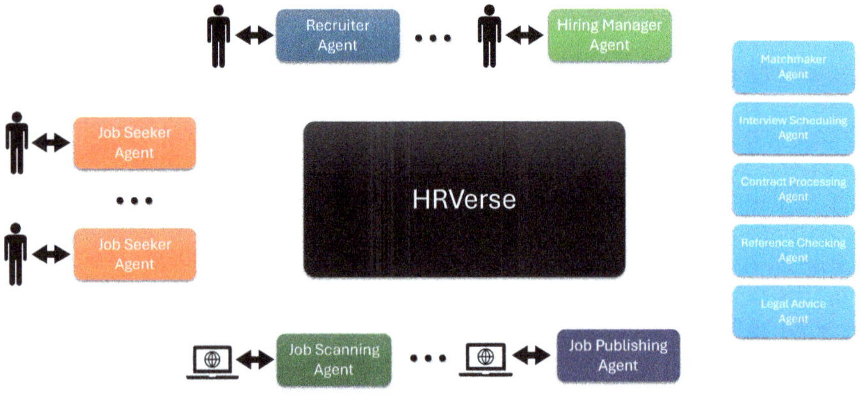

Fig. 10.2 Overview of an HRVerse agentic ecosystem

Similar to the TravelVerse, a successful HRVerse platform can profoundly impact the HR landscape by automating tasks and transactions that currently require significant human effort and coordination. While humans will remain the decision-makers, AI agents can simplify options and choices for both job seekers and hiring managers.

The platform can also be used for mass recruitment campaigns across industries (e.g. seasonal jobs in agriculture, tourism) or facilitate work across countries with special visa requirements, streamlining and simplifying current processes.

10.5 The Future of Agentic Ecosystems

The concepts discussed can be replicated across various verticals to create agentic ecosystems that transact a wide range of goods and services, from property and telecommunications to health and financial services. In the financial services sector, we anticipate significant growth in payments conducted by agents, with some companies already offering agent wallets to facilitate these transactions. Additionally, cryptocurrencies are expected to receive a boost from agentic ecosystems, similar to the growth seen with meme currencies.

For AgentVerses to be trusted, a certain degree of regulation and central authority is necessary, whether operated by private or public entities. While these are still early days, the success of nascent AgentVerses could lead to a proliferation of the concept. This brings us to the idea of an X-Verse, where different digital worlds coexist with various purposes and experiences. Some of these worlds may be dominated by transacting AI agents, while others focus on human entertainment, potentially cohabited by both humans and AI agents.

Last but not least, assuming AI agents can be treated as digital labour one may envisage agentic ecosystems devoted to trading into agent capabilities themselves. Similar to Software as a Service (SaaS), the notion of Agentic Services may develop not only targeting the productivity tool market but also the overall world labour market (e.g. hiring of AI agents for customer service or other jobs similar to human labour hiring). How these services will be charged remains an open question. Suggestions to date include basing it on the amount of work completed, a discount of the equivalent human salary, the amount of time it took to complete work, or charging per conversation/answer provided by the AI agent.

Chapter 11
Robotics Revolution

AI agents can be understood as progressing through two waves of technological innovation, each with significant business transformation potential. The first wave, currently underway, focuses on virtual or digital agents. This wave has been explored extensively throughout the chapters of this book, highlighting how these AI agents are reshaping digital interactions, automation, and decision-making processes.

The second wave is poised to bring even more profound change. It centres on AI agents embodied in physical forms: robots capable of perceiving, acting, and engaging with the physical world. This development will unlock an unprecedented range of applications, marking the beginning of the long-anticipated revolution in robotics.

C. Voudouris, *Autonomic Business Transformation*, Management for Professionals, https://doi.org/10.1007/978-3-032-01415-3_11

In this chapter, we will explore the current landscape of so-called embodied AI, the influence of large language model (LLM) agents in this space, and how organizations can harness robotics today to drive autonomic business transformation.

11.1 Autonomy in Robotics

Robotics in manufacturing has a long and enduring legacy of enhancing productivity and driving automation. In Chap. 5, we explored the example of an automated EV factory, where robots play a central role in operations. Since the 2000s, the use of robotics has expanded beyond manufacturing into other sectors, notably with the emergence of autonomous vehicles and drones across land, air, and sea domains.

The transformative potential of these technologies is evident in various applications: drones are now widely used across multiple industries, autopilot systems are becoming standard in automotive contexts, and innovations in rail, maritime, and shipping sectors continue to accelerate.

For instance, the Port of Rotterdam anticipates that by the 2030s, marine traffic entering and exiting the port could be autonomously managed [251]. Fully autonomous metro systems, operating without drivers, have already been successfully deployed in several regions [169]. In logistics, warehouse robots are routinely used by major retailers such as Ocado and Amazon [180]. On the battlefield, drones, both aerial and maritime, are reshaping modern warfare, offering a glimpse into how future conflicts may be fought and won.

Despite these advancements, today's robotics systems are still far from achieving full autonomy. Most continue to operate under human supervision, with critical decision-making and tasking largely handled by humans rather than AI agents. While deep learning and neural networks have significantly advanced image recognition, even the most sophisticated robots, such as those developed by Boston Dynamics, rely heavily on algorithms focused on sensor integration, dynamics, and control. AI plays a crucial role in the stack, but it does not yet dominate every layer of robotic intelligence.

The author of this book has previously explored the application of AI techniques to autonomous mobile robots, yielding promising results [252]. However, for anyone involved in developing autonomous robotic systems, it quickly becomes clear how challenging it is to deploy robots in unpredictable, real-world environments: beyond the controlled conditions of a lab and beyond narrowly defined tasks in scope and duration.

While AI has significantly advanced the processing of sensor data, improved the accuracy of image recognition, and, with the advent of large language models (LLMs), greatly enhanced natural language interaction, the physical aspects of robotics remain a major hurdle. Tasks such as navigating unstructured environments or manipulating objects with human-like dexterity continue to pose substantial challenges.

As with AI agents, robotics may be on the cusp of a new wave of innovation, driven by the convergence and maturation of several enabling technologies. These

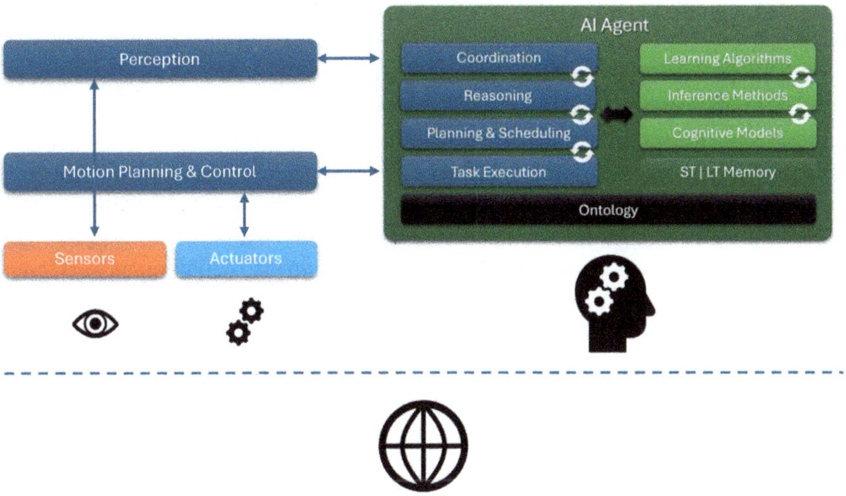

Fig. 11.1 Integrating AI agents into robots

advances are paving the way for robots that can operate effectively in real-world settings and within broader enterprise contexts.

A high-level architecture for integrating AI agents into robotics is illustrated in Fig. 11.1. In this model, sensors collect environmental data, which is processed by a perception module that transforms raw inputs into meaningful patterns. This enables the AI agent to construct a model of the external world and evaluate the consequences of its actions. Based on its objectives, the agent engages in reasoning, planning, and task scheduling, which may lead to actions such as navigating through space or manipulating objects.

These high-level decisions are translated by a motion planning and control module into low-level commands for the robot's actuators. The resulting physical actions alter the environment, generating new sensory inputs that feed back into the system, creating a continuous loop of perception, reasoning, and action.

Although the equivalent of large language models (LLMs) in the form of Large Motion and Vision Models is still in its early stages [253, 254], one can envision a future where these models evolve and converge, integrating language, perception, and motion into a unified framework or a coordinated set of models. This convergence could ultimately pave the way for intelligent, autonomous robots capable of operating effectively in real-world environments.

11.2 Extracting Value from Robotics

Autonomic operations will take on new dimensions as AI agents and robotics converge into intelligent autonomous machines, capable of interacting with the physical world and moving beyond the confines of purely digital environments. While today's AI agents primarily impact office-based and professional work, intelligent autonomous machines are poised to transform manual and blue-collar work, particularly in unstructured environments that have so far been less susceptible to automation than the controlled settings of factories.

In general, the cost of a device is a function of its complexity and size. Assuming humanoid robots reach a level of complexity and scale comparable to that of a motorcycle or a car, their prices are likely to decrease with mass production, eventually becoming affordable for average households and businesses.

A new industry will emerge around the manufacturing, deployment, servicing, and upgrading of these robots. Companies with expertise in automotive or home appliances are well-positioned to enter this market from a hardware perspective. Automotive firms such as Tesla and Hyundai already have a strong presence in robotics, with Hyundai (through Boston Dynamics) also showing early signs of successful commercialization. On the software side, tech vendors will play a key role in developing core operating systems and adding value through programmable skills and functionalities built on top of the hardware platform. This evolution could mirror the PC industry, where a standard hardware and OS foundation supports a wide range of applications tailored to diverse needs.

Leasing models may help reduce the cost of ownership, while specialized autonomous vehicles, such as self-driving cars and trains, represent the next evolutionary step, offering alternatives to today's non-autonomous transport systems.

A comprehensive autonomic strategy should consider both digital and physical (embodied) AI agents. Organizations can begin by automating processes, decisions, and tasks, and eventually augment their workforce with robots as these become more accessible and cost-effective, potentially reaching price points similar to current vehicles or industrial machinery. Within a 10- to 20-year timeframe, we may see the emergence of hybrid AI workforces, where virtual agents and physical robots collaborate to complete projects with minimal human supervision.

These robots could take on high-risk tasks in hazardous environments, such as post-nuclear accident zones, deep-sea operations, and extraterrestrial missions for mining or construction on the Moon or Mars, where human presence is either dangerous or impractical.

However, progress in these areas will not be uniform or immediate. Significant engineering challenges remain across multiple domains, including mechanical and electrical engineering, sensor technologies, materials science, energy management, and battery efficiency. Overcoming these hurdles will be essential to enabling robots to operate reliably over extended periods, with minimal recharging and increasing levels of autonomy.

Below are the key domains where robotics can be effectively leveraged to deliver value in the short term:

- **Industrial robots**:

  Robots used in manufacturing, performing tasks such as painting, welding, and component handling, have been deployed for decades. They continue to deliver tangible benefits by improving quality and automating production lines.

- **Domestic robots**:
  From robotic lawn mowers to vacuum cleaners, robotics is increasingly finding applications in home environments. As costs decline and efficiency improves, these robots will become more common in everyday domestic tasks.
- **Transport and logistics robots**:
  Self-driving cars and trains, drones, and warehouse robots are already demonstrating significant potential. These technologies are being actively deployed in logistics and supply chain operations, with autonomy levels advancing rapidly.
- **Military robots**:
  While military applications raise important ethical considerations, certain use cases, such as bomb disposal and surveillance, are already in use and generally considered non-contentious.
- **Retail and service robots**:
  In sectors like healthcare, hospitality, entertainment, and retail, robots can deliver substantial enterprise value. Examples include surgical assistance in hospitals, tour guiding in public venues, performance roles in entertainment, and customer service tasks such as checkout and delivery in retail.
- **Agricultural robots**:
  Robotics in agriculture can enhance efficiency in tasks such as seeding, watering, weeding, and harvesting. With several enabling technologies maturing, this sector is poised for significant progress.

Figure 11.2 illustrates these primary areas where robotics can be applied today to extract value.

11.3 Challenges Facing Today's Robotic Technologies

Despite rapid advancements, current robotic technologies face several significant challenges that limit their broader adoption:

- **Unpredictable real-world environments:** Robots often struggle to operate reliably in dynamic, unstructured environments. Unforeseen events can disrupt their operations, and unlike humans, robots are typically unable to adapt in real time to such variability.
- **Limited integration of AI agents:** As discussed earlier in this chapter, the integration of AI agents into robotic systems remains limited. In many domains, human supervision is still essential to ensure tasks are completed successfully and to manage exceptions that arise during operation.
- **Need for improved human–robot interaction:** In certain contexts, particularly in healthcare and social care, robots must interact closely with humans to be effective. For example, assisting patients or the elderly requires a level of empathy, adaptability, and communication that remains challenging for current systems.

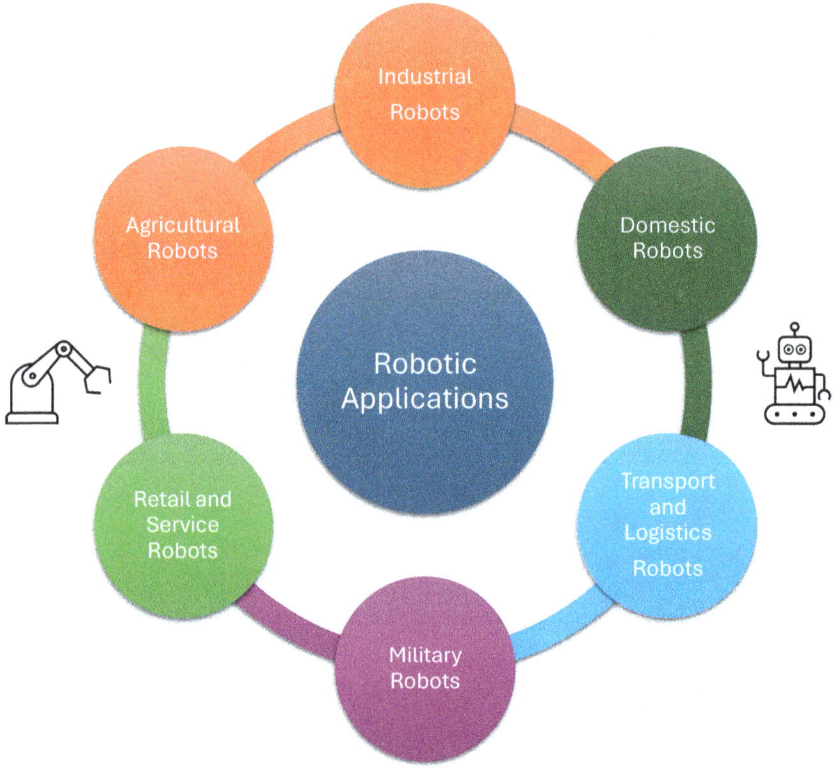

Fig. 11.2 Robotic applications that can be leveraged today

- **Safety, security, and ethical considerations:** The integration of robots into society raises important safety and ethical questions. These concerns must be addressed proactively and incorporated into the design and R&D phases, rather than being treated as afterthoughts.

To date, many of these challenges have not been fully addressed by reinforcement learning (RL) or other machine learning techniques. Overcoming them may require a combination of RL with large-scale models in language, perception, and motion, augmented by neuro-symbolic approaches that can better navigate the complexity of real-world environments. The author has previously applied a neuro-symbolic approach based on fuzzy logic in the context of autonomous mobile robots [255]. The method enabled the system to interpret its environment through symbolic reasoning, which was then rapidly translated into numerical and effective motion planning and control though a fuzzy decision tree architecture.

Along with new algorithmic approaches, a major mind shift, as discussed in the following section, may play an equally critical role in accelerating this journey towards truly autonomous, intelligent robotic systems.

11.4 Humanoid vs Specialized Robots

The future of robotics does not necessarily lie in humanoid forms, nor should that be the primary goal. Humans have been shaped by evolution to survive in their natural habitat, not to efficiently perform tasks like transporting goods in warehouses or conducting surgical procedures. Yet, the robotics industry has long been captivated by the idea of humanoid robots, with recent examples such as Tesla's Optimus robot [264] and Figure's "Figure 02" autonomous humanoid robot [265] continuing this trend.

Instead, robot design should be optimized for the specific task at hand, tailored to the function and the environment in which the task must be performed. Striving to replicate human balance, dexterity, or reasoning may be an unnecessarily complex challenge, especially when such capabilities are not required for tasks like pallet transport or highway navigation. Just as airplanes do not need flapping wings to fly, mimicking nature should not be the objective, and in many cases, it may even hinder the development of practical robotic solutions.

The focus should shift towards specialized robots with increasing degrees of autonomy, capable of executing tasks efficiently in complex and unpredictable real-world settings. Moving beyond the humanoid paradigm opens the door to designing solutions that are viable today, not decades from now. Generative AI and AI-driven design tools can be harnessed to create highly optimized robotic forms [266], purpose-built to outperform humans in specific tasks.

This is not to say that humanoid designs have no place, particularly in environments built for human use, such as homes, offices, and cell stations in factories [267]. However, humanoid form should be the outcome of a design process that prioritizes function over form, not the starting point. By doing so, we can accelerate the practical benefits of the robotics revolution and deploy useful systems much sooner.

Chapter 12
Epilogue

The advent of autonomic business is inevitable as technologies like AI agents reach maturity levels suitable for everyday use. Combined with other technologies such as those explored in earlier chapters, they become even more powerful. These technologies harness recent innovations across diverse fields and disciplines to deliver new user experiences and create a machine layer that underpins most aspects of modern life, effecting changes not seen since the advent of the Internet and mobile technologies. With agentic ecosystems and robotics the future is going to be a different world to that experienced to date both for individual and businesses.

C. Voudouris, *Autonomic Business Transformation*, Management for Professionals, https://doi.org/10.1007/978-3-032-01415-3_12

Because of this fundamental shift where humans have to share the workplace with intelligent machines, this time the autonomic business transformation also raises philosophical and existential concerns, similar to those seen with advancements in nuclear technology. It is intriguing when public figures quote percentages on the likelihood of AI turning bad or good, as if they can predict such outcomes. One certainty is that the purpose of developing new technologies should be clearly focused on serving a human-centric vision of the enterprise and the world, rather than confusing the ability of machines to think with their ability to set their own high-level vision and goals.

Machines should not be treated in isolation from humans or declared a separate species antagonizing humans because they can reason, plan, and achieve their goals through task execution. More importantly, they cannot exist without ultimately serving some goal or purpose relevant to humans. Even a utopian or dystopian vision where machines attain physical embodiment in the form of humanoid robots, as explored in the previous chapter, with some form of consciousness taking over the planet is simply a science fiction conversation at this stage. It undermines the significance and seriousness of already substantiated risks to humans, such as climate change, nuclear proliferation, the rise of autocratic regimes, and social media manipulation.

This is not to say that oversight and control of AI systems should not be applied and improved, as explored in past chapters. Rather, it stresses the need for a human-centric approach to autonomic business and AI agents, where self-managing, self-adapting technologies ultimately serve human goals.

It is safe to assume that AI agents will shape the upcoming wave of innovation [256], with autonomic business concepts starting to emerge and gradually dominate as the next wave after digital business. Early studies on the rise of agentic [257] and generative AI [258] suggest that changes will be faster and more profound than previous waves, with those missing out potentially facing a huge productivity gap and a mountain to climb later on. Participating as individuals and enterprises is the best way to shape the evolution of these powerful tools and mitigate any risks associated with their application.

The degree of resistance to autonomic business is likely to be influenced by demographics, geography, and wider socio-economic factors. In some ways, the ground for autonomic business adoption is more fertile compared to previous waves. Executives are more exposed to new AI technologies through personal experiences, and a younger workforce is more open to the idea of autonomic operations as they are more amenable to sharing personal data and information online and through social media.

AI agents will be pervasive and quickly proliferate as today's application vendors move to offering agentic user experiences and develop multi-agent approaches to autonomously execute and troubleshoot even the most complex workflows. Businesses should explore areas of opportunity now, develop use cases, and progress with AI agent design and piloting. At the same time, businesses should commence to formulate a comprehensive autonomic business strategy and principles to set the guidelines and stay at the forefront of this unprecedented wave of transformation.

Starting work on longer-term strategies is equally, if not more, important than experimenting with AI agents. The right decisions at the start of the journey can provide the right foundations, evolve capabilities in a coordinated fashion, and control risks more effectively. The journey will bring unexpected challenges, as was the case with previous waves, and past journeys such as cloud and digital transformations haven't been fully completed. A review of past cloud and digital plans through the lens of autonomic business should be considered. For example, reengineering legacy applications to be cloud-native or adopting web technologies can be a step that becomes obsolete when these applications can be replaced by AI agents executing advanced versions of RPA that can adapt to the intricacies of these legacy applications, delivering on user goals and shielding them from navigating a myriad of applications and interfaces to achieve the same results.

Lastly, autonomic business should not be limited to operations. While AI agents represent tremendous potential in creating self-managing and self-adapting operations, the larger potential lies in agentic ecosystems and AgentVerses. When these agent-driven marketplaces emerge and combine with technologies like digital contracts and currencies, they can set the foundation for an agentic web economy that may eclipse current human-driven markets. The ability to offer and buy services in such an agentic web economy may achieve similar importance to the web presence in the early e-commerce days.

Ultimately, autonomic business will be judged by its contribution to creating a better place for humans, where AI agents create frictionless experiences for us in pursuing our goals and desires. Much of today's insecurity with AI, and more specifically AI agents, comes from their increasing ability to perform some of our current tasks and jobs. We have increasingly defined ourselves by the work we do and the positions we hold in organizations. In that race, we often deprioritized the importance of lifelong learning, participating in politics to better our societies, expressing ourselves through the arts and written works, debating with others to advance understanding, and investing time to guide the next generation to avoid our mistakes. Who associates a profession or position with Plato, Aristotle, or Socrates? They were known simply as philosophers or polymaths.

AI agents do not deprive us of pursuing or substituting any of these activities. Instead, they create more space and time to deepen our understanding of ourselves and our world. It is important to distribute more fairly the wealth created by the unprecedented levels of productivity and innovation to come. Otherwise, a new autonomic-type divide may emerge, where businesses and individuals benefiting from increased automation create a stranglehold and quasi-monopoly on the underlying models and algorithms. Movements such as open-sourcing AI technologies and frontier models are critical to avoid such extremes.

In time, the next wave of technologies will take over from AI as autonomic business and agents are woven into the fabric of societies and economies. It is hard to predict what will come next, but several existing candidates, such as quantum computing, hold significant promise. We are conditioned to think that because the last few waves focused on information and communication technologies, the next ones will be as well. This may be proven entirely false, with breakthroughs in mathematics, physics, energy production, or biology heralding new waves and eras. The destination is not always as important as the journey. Many of us enjoy the journey as well. Having started on AI algorithms and agent R&D back in 1995 as my first job in the telecommunications industry, I have certainly enjoyed this 30-year journey and hopefully accurately captured my experiences and knowledge in this book so the current and next generation of practitioners and executives can learn from the experiences and learnings of the past. Someone may claim that AI may be able to write similar books in a few years, and that may come true, but it will always be original human thought that comes through these books too.

Going back to my Greek roots, I always think of Homer, Plato, Aristotle, and Socrates, whose teachings I studied through my school years. Their thoughts in written form have survived and travelled through the ages. These thoughts are now encoded in the weights of neural networks, propagated and amplified through countless inferences taking place every millisecond, benefiting the work and life of other humans. This is a remarkable achievement for our human species to be admired and embraced until the next one which with the help of AI agents can be even greater…

References

1. Raskino, M., Lopez, J., Furlonger, D., Smith, S., Uzureau, C., Poitevin, H., Scheibenreif, D., Sicular, S., Brethenoux, E., Sau, M., Shotton, L., & Kerremans, M. (2022). *Autonomous business is the next tech-enabled strategic growth curve for pioneer enterprises*. Gartner. https://www.gartner.com/en/documents/4013326
2. Shardt, Y. A. W. (2025). *Automation engineering*. Springer. https://doi.org/10.1007/978-3-031-92394-4
3. Jones, N. (2024). AI now beats humans at basic tasks — New benchmarks are needed, says major report. *Nature*. https://www.nature.com/articles/d41586-024-01087-4
4. Dehraj, P., & Sharma, A. (2021). A review on architecture and models for autonomic software systems. *The Journal of Supercomputing, 77*, 388–417. https://doi.org/10.1007/s11227-020-03268-0
5. Jones, N., Brethenoux, E., & Cearley, D. (2021). *Top strategic technology trends for 2022: Autonomic systems*. Gartner. https://www.gartner.com/en/documents/4006930
6. Franklin, S., & Graesser, A. (1996). Is it an agent, or just a program?: A taxonomy for autonomous agents. In J. P. Müller, M. J. Wooldridge, & N. R. Jennings (Eds.), *Intelligent agents III: Agent theories, architectures, and languages (ATAL 1996)* (Lecture Notes in Computer Science) (Vol. 1193, pp. 21–35). Springer. https://doi.org/10.1007/BFb0013570
7. Wooldridge, M. (1997). Agent-based computing. *The Knowledge Engineering Review, 12*(3), 1–39.
8. Cambridge University Press. (2025). *Agency*. Cambridge English Dictionary. Retrieved May 25, 2025, from https://dictionary.cambridge.org/dictionary/english/agency
9. Cambridge University Press. (2025). *Autonomy*. Cambridge English Dictionary. Retrieved May 25, 2025, from https://dictionary.cambridge.org/dictionary/english/autonomy
10. Landau, I. D., Lozano, R., M'Saad, M., & Karimi, A. (2011). *Adaptive control: Algorithms, analysis and applications*. Springer.
11. Benioff, M. (2024). *Agentic AI reshapes the workforce*. Salesforce Newsroom. Retrieved May 25, 2025, from https://www.salesforce.com/news/stories/agentic-ai-reshapes-workforce/
12. Nadella, S. (2025). *Meet your new AI teammate: Microsoft sees humans as 'agent bosses', upending the workplace*. GeekWire. Retrieved May 25, 2025, from https://www.geekwire.com/2025/meet-your-new-ai-teammate-microsoft-sees-humans-as-agent-bosses-upending-the-workplace/
13. Altman, S. (2024). *Reflections*. Sam Altman's Blog. Retrieved May 25, 2025, from https://blog.samaltman.com/reflections
14. Gupta, R., Tiwari, S., & Chaudhary, P. (2024). *Generative AI: Techniques, models and applications*. Springer. https://doi.org/10.1007/978-3-031-82062-5

C. Voudouris, *Autonomic Business Transformation*, Management for Professionals, https://doi.org/10.1007/978-3-032-01415-3

15. Gadatsch, A. (2023). *Business process management: Analysis, modelling, optimisation and controlling of processes* (10th ed.). Springer Vieweg. https://doi.org/10.1007/978-3-658-41584-6
16. Langmann, C., & Turi, D. (2022). *Robotic process automation (RPA)—Digitization and automation of business processes*. Springer Vieweg. https://doi.org/10.1007/978-3-658-38692-4
17. Kerremans, M., & Cearley, D. (2022). *Building a digital future: Autonomic business operations*. Gartner. https://www.pega.com/gartner-autonomic-business-operations
18. IBM Corporation. (2021). *Enterprise governance*. IBM Documentation. Retrieved May 26, 2025, from https://www.ibm.com/docs/en/cloud-paks/cp-data/5.1.x?topic=enterprise-governance
19. UK Parliament. (2006). *Companies Act 2006, Section 155*. https://www.legislation.gov.uk/ukpga/2006/46/section/155
20. Schwab, K. (2017). *The fourth industrial revolution*. Portfolio Penguin.
21. European Parliament. (2015). *Industry 4.0*. European Parliamentary Research Service.
22. Breque, M., De Nul, L., & Petridis, A. (2021). *Industry 5.0: Towards a sustainable, human-centric and resilient European industry*. Publications Office of the European Union.
23. Scheibenreif, D., & Raskino, M. (2023). *When machines become customers: Ready or not, AI enabled non-human customers are coming to your business. How you adapt will make or break your future*. Gartner.
24. European Commission. (2025). *EU launches InvestAI initiative to mobilise €200 billion for artificial intelligence development*. Representation of the European Commission in Luxembourg. https://luxembourg.representation.ec.europa.eu/actualites-et-evenements/actualites/eu-launches-investai-initiative-mobilise-eu200-billion-investment-artificial-intelligence-2025-02-11_en
25. CB Insights. (2024). *Future of the workforce: How AI agents will transform enterprise workflows*. CB Insights Research. https://www.cbinsights.com/research/report/future-workforce-ai-agents/
26. Casper, S., Bailey, L., Hunter, R., Ezell, C., Cabalé, E., Gerovitch, M., Slocum, S., Wei, K., Jurkovic, N., Khan, A., Christoffersen, P. J. K., Ozisik, A. P., Trivedi, R., Hadfield-Menell, D., & Kolt, N. (2025). *The AI agent index*. arXiv preprint arXiv:2502.01635. https://arxiv.org/abs/2502.01635
27. Deloitte. (2024). *Autonomous generative AI agents: Under development*. Deloitte Insights. https://www2.deloitte.com/us/en/insights/industry/technology/technology-media-and-telecom-predictions/2025/autonomous-generative-ai-agents-still-under-development.html
28. Boston Consulting Group. (2024). *AI agents: What they are and their business impact*. https://www.bcg.com/capabilities/artificial-intelligence/ai-agents
29. Osterwalder, A., & Pigneur, Y. (2010). *Business model generation: A handbook for visionaries, game changers, and challengers*. Wiley.
30. Wooldridge, M. (2009). *An introduction to MultiAgent systems*. Wiley.
31. FIPA. (2005). *IEEE computer society FIPA standards committee*. Foundation for Intelligent Physical Agents. https://www.fipa.org
32. Jennings, N. R., Faratin, P., Norman, T. J., O'Brien, P., Weigand, M. E., Voudouris, C., Alty, J. L., Miah, T., & Mamdani, E. H. (1996). ADEPT: Managing business processes using intelligent agents. In *Proceedings of the BCS expert systems 96 conference (Intelligent systems integration programme track), Cambridge, United Kingdom* (pp. 5–23).
33. Odgers, B., & Voudouris, C. (1997). Using agents to manage business resources and services. In *Proceedings of the sixth international interfaces conference (interfaces '97)* (pp. 183–186).
34. O'Brien, P., Wiegand, M., Odgers, B., Voudouris, C., & Judge, D. (1997). Using software agents for business process management. *British Telecommunications Engineering Journal, 15*(4), 326–333.
35. British Telecommunications. (1997). *ABW_Zeus: Innovation in business process management*. British Computer Society IT Awards 1997.
36. Luck, M., McBurney, P., & Preist, C. (2003). *Agent technology: Enabling next generation computing—A roadmap for agent-based computing. AgentLink*. University of Southampton.

37. Luck, M., McBurney, P., & Preist, C. (2004). A manifesto for agent technology: Towards next generation computing. *Autonomous Agents and Multi-Agent Systems, 9*(3), 203–252. https://doi.org/10.1023/B:AGNT.0000038027.29035.7c
38. FIPA. (2002). *FIPA communicative act library specification*. Foundation for Intelligent Physical Agents. https://www.fipa.org/specs/fipa00037/SC00037J.html
39. Bellifemine, F., Caire, G., Poggi, A., & Rimassa, G. (2003). JADE: A software framework for developing multi-agent applications. *International Journal of Autonomous Agents and Multi-Agent Systems, 7*(1–2), 91–120. https://doi.org/10.1023/A:1022146019586
40. Nwana, H. S., Ndumu, D. T., Lee, L. C., & Collis, J. C. (1999). ZEUS: A toolkit for building distributed multi-agent systems. *Applied Artificial Intelligence, 13*(1–2), 129–185. https://doi.org/10.1080/088395199117289
41. British Telecommunications plc. (2002). *ZEUS Agent Toolkit* (Open Source Edition). SourceForge. https://sourceforge.net/projects/zeusagent/
42. European Commission. (2001). *AgentCities.RTD: A European Research and technology development initiative*. IST Programme, Information Society Technologies. https://cordis.europa.eu/project/id/IST-2000-28385
43. BT Group and University College London (UCL). (2003). *Generative software development initiative*. Collaborative research project at BT Adastral Park.
44. Finkelstein, A., Mihailescu, P., & Savignac, M. (2003). Weaving aspects into web service orchestrations. In *Proceedings of the 2nd International Conference on Aspect-Oriented Software Development* (pp. 100–109). ACM Press.
45. Elliot, J. (1981). System X: The British digital switching system. *IEEE Communications Magazine, 19*(6), 12–18. https://doi.org/10.1109/MCOM.1981.1094467
46. Virginas, B., Voudouris, C., Owusu, G., & Anim-Ansah, G. (2003). ARMS collaborator—Intelligent agents using markets to organise resourcing in modern enterprises. *BT Technology Journal, 21*(4), 59–64.
47. Tsang, E. P. K., Gosling, T., Virginas, B., Voudouris, C., Owusu, G., & Liu, W. (2008). Retractable contract network for empowerment in workforce scheduling. *Multiagent and Grid Systems, 4*(1), 25–44.
48. Brown, T., et al. (2020). Language models are few-shot learners. *Advances in Neural Information Processing Systems, 33*, 1877–1901.
49. Anthropic. (2024). *Introducing the model context protocol*. https://www.anthropic.com/news/model-context-protocol
50. Google. (2025). *Announcing Agent2Agent protocol: A new era of agent interoperability*. https://blog.google/products/google-cloud/next-2025/
51. LaPierre, R. (2025). *Introduction to quantum computing* (2nd ed.). Springer. https://doi.org/10.1007/978-3-031-90731-9
52. Arshi, O., & Chaudhary, A. (2024). Overview of artificial general intelligence (AGI). In *Artificial general intelligence (AGI) security* (pp. 1–26). Springer. https://link.springer.com/chapter/10.1007/978-981-97-3222-7_1
53. Goertzel, B., et al. (2024). *Artificial general intelligence: 17th international conference, AGI 2024, Seattle, WA, USA, Proceedings*. Springer. https://link.springer.com/book/10.1007/978-3-031-65572-2
54. Saad, W., Bennis, M., & Chen, M. (Eds.). (2020). *6G: The road to the future wireless technologies 2030*. IEEE Press.
55. Lee, L. H., et al. (2022). All one needs to know about Metaverse: A complete survey on technological singularity, virtual ecosystem, and research agenda. *Journal of Network and Computer Applications, 197*, 103348. https://doi.org/10.1016/j.jnca.2021.103348
56. Miller, D. A. B. (2010). Optical computing: A perspective. *Proceedings of the IEEE, 88*(9), 1554–1569. https://doi.org/10.1109/JPROC.2010.2060050

57. Biamonte, J., Wittek, P., Pancotti, N., Rebentrost, P., Wiebe, N., & Lloyd, S. (2017). Quantum machine learning. *Nature, 549*(7671), 195–202. https://doi.org/10.1038/nature23474
58. Gago Huerta, S., & Recio, C. (2025). *The next frontier after AI agents: Quantum artificial intelligence*. Moody's Analytics. https://www.moodys.com/web/en/us/insights/resources/next-frontier-after-ai-agents.pdf
59. SAE International. (2021). *Taxonomy and definitions for terms related to driving automation systems for on-road motor vehicles (SAE standard J3016_202104)*. SAE International. https://doi.org/10.4271/J3016_202104
60. Kopetz, H. (2022). An architecture for safe driving automation. In J.-F. Raskin & K. Chatterjee (Eds.), *Principles of systems design* (pp. 61–84). Springer. https://doi.org/10.1007/978-3-031-22337-2_4
61. Zhang, Y., Goverde, R. M. P., & Lodewijks, G. (2020). A review on railway automation and train operation levels. *Journal of Modern Transportation, 28*, 1–18. https://doi.org/10.1007/s40534-020-00214-2
62. Voudouris, C., Owusu, G., Dorne, R., & Lesaint, D. (2008). *Service chain management: Technology innovation for the service business*. Springer. https://doi.org/10.1007/978-3-540-75504-3
63. Saracco, R. (2022). *Digital humans: Life in the Metaverse*. IEEE Future Directions. https://cmte.ieee.org/futuredirections/2022/11/11/digital-humans-life-in-the-metaverse/.
64. PaymanAI. (2025). *AI agents that delegate tasks to humans and pay them*. Retrieved May 26, 2025, from https://pay-manai.com
65. Hamilton, D. (2025). *What is Gibberlink mode, AI's secret language?* Forbes. Retrieved May 26, 2025, from https://www.forbes.com/sites/dianehamilton/2025/02/25/what-is-gibberlink-mode-ais-secret-language-and-way-of-communicating/
66. Drew, L. (2024). *Elon Musk's Neuralink brain chip: What scientists think of first human trial*. Nature. Retrieved May 26, 2025, from https://www.nature.com/articles/d41586-024-00304-4
67. Temkin, M. (2024). *Why AI agent startup/dev/agents commanded a massive $56M seed round at a $500M valuation*. TechCrunch. https://techcrunch.com/2024/11/28/ai-agent-startup-dev-agents-has-raised-a-massive-56m-seed-round-at-a-500m-valuation/
68. Park, J. S., Zou, C. Q., Shaw, A., Hill, B. M., Cai, C., Morris, M. R., Willer, R., Liang, P., & Bernstein, M. S. (2024). *Generative agent simulations of 1,000 people*. arXiv preprint arXiv:2411.10109. https://arxiv.org/abs/2411.10109
69. Zeff, M. (2025). Nvidia's AI avatar sat on my computer screen and weirded me out. TechCrunch.https://techcrunch.com/2025/01/09/nvidias-ai-avatar-sat-on-my-computer-screen-and-weirded-me-out/
70. OpenAI. (2024). *Hello GPT-4o*. https://openai.com/index/hello-gpt-4o
71. xAI. (2023). *Grok*. https://x.ai/grok
72. Chandrasekaran, A. (2024). *Hype cycle for generative AI, 2024*. Gartner. https://www.gartner.com/en/articles/hype-cycle-for-genai
73. Schmidt, E. (2025). *The AI revolution is underhyped [video]*. TED. https://www.youtube.com/watch?v=id4YRO7G0wE
74. McGrath, R. G. (2013). The pace of technology adoption is speeding up. *Harvard Business Review*. https://hbr.org/2013/11/the-pace-of-technology-adoption-is-speeding-up
75. Shaw, F. X. (2025). *Microsoft build 2025: The age of AI agents and building the open agentic web*. The Official Microsoft Blog. Retrieved May 26, 2025, from https://blogs.microsoft.com/blog/2025/05/19/microsoft-build-2025-the-age-of-ai-agents-and-building-the-open-agentic-web/
76. Meta. (2025). *Introducing the Meta AI App: A new way to access your AI assistant*. Meta Newsroom. Retrieved May 26, 2025, from https://about.fb.com/news/2025/04/introducing-meta-ai-app-new-way-access-ai-assistant/
77. Google. (2025). *Google I/O 2025: News and announcements*. The Keyword Blog. Retrieved May 26, 2025, from https://blog.google/technology/developers/google-io-2025-collection/

78. Amazon AGI Labs. (2025). *Introducing Nova act: A new model for building reliable web agents*. Amazon Science Blog. Retrieved May 26, 2025, from https://labs.amazon.science/blog/nova-act
79. Hecht, A. (2025). *AI agents redefine work with NVIDIA AI enterprise*. NVIDIA Blog. Retrieved May 26, 2025, from https://blogs.nvidia.com/blog/ai-enterprise-agents/
80. Salesforce. (2024). *Salesforce unveils Agentforce—What AI was meant to be*. Salesforce Newsroom. Retrieved May 26, 2025, from https://www.salesforce.com/news/press-releases/2024/09/12/agentforce-announcement/
81. Huang, S., & Grady, P. (2024). *The new ideas needed for AGI*. Sequoia Capital. https://www.sequoiacap.com/article/new-ideas-for-agi/
82. Heaven, W. D. (2023). *Geoffrey Hinton tells us why he's now scared of the tech he helped build*. MIT Technology Review. Retrieved May 26, 2025, from https://www.technologyreview.com/2023/05/02/1072528/geoffrey-hinton-google-why-scared-ai/
83. Sutskever, I. (2024). *Data is the 'fossil fuel' of A.I., says OpenAI co-founder Ilya Sutskever*. Observer. https://observer.com/2024/12/openai-cofounder-ilya-sutskever-ai-data-peak/
84. Russakovsky, O., Deng, J., Su, H., Krause, J., Satheesh, S., Ma, S., Huang, Z., Karpathy, A., Khosla, A., Bernstein, M., Berg, A. C., & Fei-Fei, L. (2015). *ImageNet large scale visual recognition challenge*. arXiv preprint arXiv:1409.0575. https://arxiv.org/abs/1409.0575
85. Silver, D., Huang, A., Maddison, C. J., Guez, A., Sifre, L., van den Driessche, G., Schrittwieser, J., Antonoglou, I., Panneershelvam, V., Lanctot, M., Dieleman, S., Grewe, D., Nham, J., Kalchbrenner, N., Sutskever, I., Lillicrap, T., Leach, M., Kavukcuoglu, K., Graepel, T., & Hassabis, D. (2016). Mastering the game of Go with deep neural networks and tree search. *Nature, 529*, 484–489. https://www.nature.com/articles/nature16961
86. Vaswani, A., Shazeer, N., Parmar, N., Uszkoreit, J., Jones, L., Gomez, A. N., Kaiser, Ł., & Polosukhin, I. (2017). Attention is all you need. In *Advances in neural information processing systems* (Vol. 30). arXiv:1706.03762.
87. Radford, A., Narasimhan, K., Salimans, T., & Sutskever, I. (2018). *Improving language understanding by generative pre-training*. OpenAI. https://www.cs.ubc.ca/~amuham01/LING530/papers/radford2018improving.pdf
88. Radford, A., Wu, J., Child, R., Luan, D., Amodei, D., & Sutskever, I. (2019). *Language models are unsupervised multitask learners*. OpenAI. https://cdn.openai.com/better-language-models/language_models_are_unsupervised_multitask_learners.pdf
89. Gates, B. (2023). *The age of AI has begun*. GatesNotes. https://www.gatesnotes.com/The-Age-of-AI-Has-Begun
90. Epoch AI. (2024). *Can AI scaling continue through 2030?* Epoch AI. https://epochai.org/blog/can-ai-scaling-continue-through-2030
91. xAI. (2024). *Colossus: The world's largest supercomputer*. xAI. https://x.ai/colossus
92. Wang, K., Zhu, J., Ren, M., Liu, Z., Li, S., Zhang, Z., Zhang, C., Wu, X., Zhan, Q., Liu, Q., & Wang, Y. (2024). *A survey on data synthesis and augmentation for large language models*. arXiv preprint arXiv:2410.12896. https://arxiv.org/abs/2410.12896
93. Dao, M. C., Das, M., Koczan, Z., & Lian, W. (2017). *The labor share of income around the world: Evidence from a panel dataset* (ADBI working paper series no. 864). Asian Development Bank Institute. https://www.adb.org/publications/labor-share-income-around-world
94. Acemoglu, D. (2024). *The simple macroeconomics of AI* (NBER working paper no. 32487). National Bureau of Economic Research. https://www.nber.org/papers/w32487
95. Guo, D., et al. (2025). *DeepSeek-R1: Incentivizing reasoning capability in LLMs via reinforcement learning*. DeepSeek-AI. arXiv preprint arXiv:2501.12948. https://arxiv.org/abs/2501.12948
96. OpenAI. (2024). *OpenAI o1: System card and model overview*. OpenAI. https://openai.com/o1/
97. OpenAI. (2025). *OpenAI o3 and o4-mini System Card*. https://openai.com/index/o3-o4-mini-system-card/

98. Poslad, S., Buckle, P., & Hadingham, R. (2000). The FIPA-OS agent platform: Open source for open standards. In *Proceedings of the 5th international conference on the practical application of intelligent agents and multi-agent technology (PAAM 2000)* (pp. 355–368).
99. Anthropic. (2024). *Claude 3 model overview*. Anthropic Documentation. https://docs.anthropic.com/en/docs/about-claude/models
100. xAI. (2024). *Grok 3 Overview*. xAI Technical Documentation. https://docs.x.ai/docs/overview
101. OpenAI. (2024). *Introducing GPT-4.1*. OpenAI Blog. https://openai.com/index/gpt-4-1/
102. Meta AI. (2024). *Llama 4: Multimodal Intelligence*. Meta AI Blog. https://ai.meta.com/blog/llama-4-multimodal-intelligence/
103. Google DeepMind. (2025). *Gemini 2.5: Our most intelligent AI model*. Google Blog. https://blog.google/technology/google-deepmind/gemini-model-thinking-updates-march-2025/
104. Wei, J., Wang, X., Schuurmans, D., Bosma, M., Ichter, B., Xia, F., Chi, E., Le, Q., & Zhou, D. (2022). *Chain-of-thought prompting elicits reasoning in large language models*. arXiv preprint arXiv:2201.11903. https://arxiv.org/abs/2201.11903
105. Yao, S., Zhao, J., Yu, D., Du, N., Shafran, I., Narasimhan, K., & Cao, Y. (2023). ReAct: Synergizing reasoning and acting in language models. In *Proceedings of the 11th international conference on learning representations (ICLR 2023)*. https://arxiv.org/abs/2210.03629
106. Barrett, A., & Weld, D. S. (1994). Partial-order planning: Evaluating possible efficiency gains. *Artificial Intelligence, 67*(1), 71–112. https://doi.org/10.1016/0004-3702(94)90012-4
107. Zhao, H., Yang, F., Shen, B., Lakkaraju, H., & Du, M. (2024). *Towards uncovering how large language model works: An explainability perspective*. arXiv preprint arXiv:2402.10688. https://arxiv.org/abs/2402.10688
108. Zaharia, M., Khattab, O., Chen, L., Davis, J. Q., Miller, H., Potts, C., Zou, J., Carbin, M., Frankle, J., Rao, N., & Ghodsi, A. (2024). *The shift from models to compound AI systems*. Berkeley AI Research Blog. https://bair.berkeley.edu/blog/2024/02/18/compound-ai-systems/
109. Patil, S. G., Zhang, T., Wang, X., & Gonzalez, J. E. (2023). *Gorilla: Large language model connected with massive APIs*. arXiv preprint arXiv:2305.15334. https://arxiv.org/abs/2305.15334
110. Schick, T., Dwivedi-Yu, J., Dessì, R., Raileanu, R., Lomeli, M., Zettlemoyer, L., Cancedda, N., & Scialom, T. (2023). *Toolformer: Language models can teach themselves to use tools*. arXiv preprint arXiv:2302.04761. https://arxiv.org/abs/2302.04761
111. Liu, Z., Hoang, T., Zhang, J., Zhu, M., Lan, T., Kokane, S., Tan, J., Yao, W., Liu, Z., Feng, Y., Murthy, R., Yang, L., Savarese, S., Niebles, J. C., Wang, H., Heinecke, S., & Xiong, C. (2024). *APIGen: Automated pipeline for generating verifiable and diverse function-calling datasets*. arXiv preprint arXiv:2406.18518. https://arxiv.org/abs/2406.18518
112. BeeAI Project Contributors. (2025). *Agent communication protocol (ACP)*. GitHub Repository. https://github.com/i-am-bee/acp
113. Proser, Z. (2025). *IBM's agent communication protocol (ACP): A technical overview for software engineers*. WorkOS Blog. https://workos.com/blog/ibm-agent-communication-protocol-acp
114. Ehtesham, A., Singh, A., Gupta, G. K., & Kumar, S. (2025). *A survey of agent interoperability protocols: Model context protocol (MCP), agent communication protocol (ACP), agent-to-agent protocol (A2A), and agent network protocol (ANP)*. arXiv preprint arXiv:2505.02279. https://arxiv.org/abs/2505.02279
115. Pretel, E., García, J. M., Cuenca, L., & García, J. (2024). Analysing the synergies between multi-agent systems and digital twins: A systematic literature review. *Information and Software Technology, 168*, 107123. https://www.sciencedirect.com/science/article/pii/S0950584924001083
116. Becker, M. C., & Pentland, B. T. (2022). Digital twin of an organization: Are you serious? In A. Marrella & B. Weber (Eds.), *Business process management workshops. LNBIP* (Vol. 436, pp. 243–254). Springer. https://link.springer.com/chapter/10.1007/978-3-030-94343-1_19
117. Dorrer, M. G. (2020). The digital twin of the business process model. *Journal of Physics: Conference Series, 1679*, 032096. https://iopscience.iop.org/article/10.1088/1742-6596/1679/3/032096/pdf

118. Zhang, J., et al. (2024). *xLAM: A family of large action models to empower AI agent systems*. arXiv preprint arXiv:2409.03215. https://arxiv.org/abs/2409.03215
119. Wang, L., Yang, F., Zhang, C., Lu, J., Qian, J., He, S., Zhao, P., Qiao, B., Huang, R., Qin, S., Su, Q., Ye, J., Zhang, Y., Lou, J.-G., Lin, Q., Rajmohan, S., Zhang, D., & Zhang, Q. (2025). *Large action models: From inception to implementation*. Microsoft. arXiv preprint arXiv:2412.10047. https://arxiv.org/abs/2412.10047
120. Orby AI. (2024). *AI agent & enterprise automation platform powered by gen AI*. https://www.orby.ai/platform
121. Wornow, M., Narayan, A., Opsahl-Ong, K., McIntyre, Q., Shah, N. H., & Ré, C. (2024). *Automating the enterprise with foundation models*. arXiv preprint arXiv:2405.03710. https://arxiv.org/abs/2405.03710
122. ITU. (2020). *IMT Vision – Framework and overall objectives of the future development of IMT for 2020 and beyond. Recommendation ITU-R M.2083-0*. International Telecommunication Union. https://www.itu.int/rec/R-REC-M.2083-0-201509-I
123. Ziegler, S., Radócz, R., Quesada Rodriguez, A., & Nieves Matheu Garcia, S. (Eds.). (2024). *Springer handbook of internet of things*. Springer.
124. Petrović, V. M. (2018). Artificial intelligence and virtual worlds—Toward human-level AI agents. *IEEE Access, 6*, 1–1. https://doi.org/10.1109/ACCESS.2018.2855970
125. Kaur, P., Taghavi, S., Tian, Z., & Shi, W. (2021). *A survey on simulators for testing self-driving cars*. arXiv preprint arXiv:2101.05337. https://arxiv.org/abs/2101.05337
126. Kyung, C.-M., Yasuura, H., Liu, Y., & Lin, Y.-L. (Eds.). (2017). *Smart sensors and systems: Innovations for medical, environmental, and IoT applications*. Springer. https://doi.org/10.1007/978-3-319-55357-3
127. Cabral, L. F., Zafar, M. I., & Ramalho, G. L. (2019). Explainable multi-agent systems through Blockchain technology. In *Advances in practical applications of agents, multi-agent systems, and complexity: The PAAMS collection* (pp. 63–75). Springer. https://doi.org/10.1007/978-3-030-19759-0_6
128. Sutton, R. S., & Barto, A. G. (2018). *Reinforcement learning: An introduction* (2nd ed.). MIT Press. https://www.andrew.cmu.edu/course/10-703/textbook/BartoSutton.pdf
129. LeCun, Y., Bengio, Y., & Hinton, G. (2015). Deep learning. *Nature, 521*(7553), 436–444. https://doi.org/10.1038/nature14539
130. Goodfellow, I., Bengio, Y., & Courville, A. (2016). Chapter 10: Sequence modeling: Recurrent and recursive nets. In *Deep learning*. MIT Press. https://www.deeplearningbook.org
131. Bhuyan, B. P., Ramdane-Cherif, A., Tomar, R., & Singh, T. P. (2024). Neuro-symbolic artificial intelligence: A survey. *Soft Computing, 28*, 1–28. https://doi.org/10.1007/s00521-024-09960-z
132. Wooldridge, M., & Jennings, N. R. (1995). Intelligent agents: Theory and practice. *The Knowledge Engineering Review, 10*(2), 115–152. https://doi.org/10.1017/S0269888900008122
133. Smith, R. G. (1980). The contract net protocol: High-level communication and control in a distributed problem solver. *IEEE Transactions on Computers, C-29*(12), 1104–1113. https://doi.org/10.1109/TC.1980.1675516
134. Yao, S., Yu, D., Zhao, J., Shafran, I., Griffiths, T. L., Cao, Y., & Narasimhan, K. (2023). *Tree of thoughts: Deliberate problem solving with large language models*. arXiv preprint arXiv:2305.10601. https://arxiv.org/abs/2305.10601
135. Wang, C., Deng, Y., Lyu, Z., Zeng, L., He, J., Yan, S., & An, B. (2024). *Q*: Improving multi-step reasoning for LLMs with deliberative planning*. arXiv preprint arXiv:2406.14283. https://doi.org/10.48550/arXiv.2406.14283
136. Zadeh, L. A. (1965). Fuzzy sets. *Information and Control, 8*(3), 338–353. https://doi.org/10.1016/S0019-9958(65)90241-X
137. Pearl, J. (1988). *Probabilistic reasoning in intelligent systems: Networks of plausible inference*. Morgan Kaufmann.
138. Lloyd, J. W. (1987). *Foundations of logic programming* (2nd ed.). Springer.

139. Apt, K. R., & Wallace, M. (2007). *Constraint logic programming using eclipse*. Cambridge University Press.
140. Aamodt, A., & Plaza, E. (1994). Case-based reasoning: Foundational issues, methodological variations, and system approaches. *AI Communications, 7*(1), 39–59. https://doi.org/10.3233/AIC-1994-7104
141. Hogan, A., Blomqvist, E., Cochez, M., d'Amato, C., Melo, G. D., Gutierrez, C., Kirrane, S., Gayo, J. E. L., Navigli, R., Neumaier, S., Polleres, A., Rula, A., Schmelzeisen, L., & Zimmermann, A. (2021). Knowledge graphs. *ACM Computing Surveys, 54*(4), 1–37. https://doi.org/10.1145/3447772
142. Nguyen, C. V., Tran, B., Lee, D., Wang, Y., Zhao, Q., Chen, T., Lin, J., & Xu, M. (2025). *A survey of small language models*. University of Oregon. arXiv preprint arXiv:2410.20011. https://arxiv.org/abs/2410.20011
143. Gong, T., Zhang, H., Zhou, M., Zhang, X., Li, P., & Wang, X. (2023). *Large multimodal models: A survey*. arXiv preprint arXiv:2311.02716. https://arxiv.org/abs/2311.02716
144. Xu, F., Hao, Q., Zong, Z., Wang, J., Zhang, Y., Wang, J., Lan, X., Gong, J., Ouyang, T., Meng, F., Shao, C., Yan, Y., Yang, Q., Song, Y., Ren, S., Hu, X., Li, Y., Feng, J., Gao, C., & Li, Y. (2025). *Towards large reasoning models: A survey of reinforced reasoning with large language models*. arXiv preprint arXiv:2501.09686. https://doi.org/10.48550/arXiv.2501.09686
145. Zhou, M., Gong, T., Wang, X., Li, P., & Zhang, H. (2024). *Large cognitive models: Toward human-level artificial intelligence*. arXiv preprint arXiv:2405.04699. https://arxiv.org/abs/2405.04699
146. Object Management Group. (2014). *Business process model and notation (BPMN) version 2.0.2*. OMG Specification. https://www.omg.org/spec/BPMN/2.0.2/About-BPMN
147. McDermott, D., Ghallab, M., Howe, A., Knoblock, C., Ram, A., Veloso, M., Weld, D., & Wilkins, D. (1998). *PDDL—The planning domain definition language. AIPS-98 planning committee memo*. Yale Center for Computational Vision and Control. http://www.cs.yale.edu/homes/dvm/papers/pddl.pdf
148. Baptiste, P., Le Pape, C., & Nuijten, W. (2001). *Constraint-based scheduling: Applying constraint programming to scheduling problems*. Springer. https://doi.org/10.1007/978-1-4613-0245-1
149. Lesaint, D., Voudouris, C., & Azarmi, N. (2000). Dynamic workforce scheduling for British Telecommunications plc. *Interfaces, 30*(1), 45–56. https://doi.org/10.1287/inte.30.1.45.11615
150. Pearl, J. (2009). *Causality: Models, reasoning, and inference* (2nd ed.). Cambridge University Press.
151. Hochreiter, S., & Schmidhuber, J. (1997). Long short-term memory. *Neural Computation, 9*(8), 1735–1780. https://doi.org/10.1162/neco.1997.9.8.1735
152. Beck, K., et al. (2001). *Manifesto for agile software development*. Agile Alliance. https://agilemanifesto.org/
153. Moura, J. M. D. (2024). *CrewAI: A framework for orchestrating collaborative AI agents*. https://github.com/crewAIInc/crewAI
154. Fourney, A., et al. (2024). *Magentic-one: A generalist multi-agent system for solving complex tasks*. arXiv preprint arXiv:2411.04468. https://arxiv.org/abs/2411.04468
155. Microsoft. (2025). *Semantic Kernel documentation*. https://learn.microsoft.com/en-us/semantic-kernel/
156. Wu, Q., et al. (2023). *AutoGen: Enabling next-gen LLM applications via multi-agent conversation*. arXiv preprint arXiv:2308.08155. https://arxiv.org/abs/2308.08155
157. Wang, J., & Duan, Z. (2024). *Agent AI with LangGraph: A modular framework for enhancing machine translation using large language models*. arXiv preprint arXiv:2412.03801. https://arxiv.org/abs/2412.03801
158. LangChain Inc. (2024). *LangGraph: A framework for building Stateful multi-agent applications*. Version v0.1.4. GitHub Repository. https://github.com/langchain-ai/langgraph
159. OpenAI. (2024). *Swarm: An educational framework for multi-agent orchestration (Version 0.1.4) [Software]*. GitHub. https://github.com/openai/swarm

160. IBM Research. (2025). *BeeAI: An open-source framework for building and orchestrating multi-agent AI systems (version 0.1.4) [software].* GitHub. https://github.com/i-am-bee/beeai-framework
161. Amazon Web Services. (2023). Amazon Bedrock Agents [Software]. https://aws.amazon.com/bedrock/agents
162. Gartner. (2023). *Hyperautomation.* https://www.gartner.com/en/information-technology/glossary/hyperautomation
163. Klarna. (2024). *Klarna AI assistant handles two-thirds of customer service chats in its first month.* Klarna Press Center. Retrieved May 27, 2025, from https://www.klarna.com/international/press/klarna-ai-assistant-handles-two-thirds-of-customer-service-chats-in-its-first-month/
164. Klarna. (2024). *Shopping made smarter: Klarna adds more AI features to its assistant powered by OpenAI.* Klarna Press Center. Retrieved May 27, 2025, from https://www.klarna.com/international/press/shopping-made-smarter-klarna-adds-more-ai-features-to-its-assistant-powered-by-openai/
165. Klarna. (2024). *Klarna's AI strategy includes decommissioning major SaaS platforms.* Klarna Press Center. Retrieved May 27, 2025, from https://www.klarna.com/international/press
166. Gurley, B., Gerstner, B., & Nadella, S. (2024). *Satya Nadella | BG2 with Bill Gurley & Brad Gerstner.* BG2 podcast. Retrieved May 27, 2025, from https://www.youtube.com/watch?v=9NtsnzRFJ_o
167. Hyundai Motor Group. (2023). *New Hyundai Motor Group Innovation Center Singapore set to transform production, R&D and customer experience.* Retrieved May 27, 2025, from https://www.hyundai.com/worldwide/en/newsroom/detail/new-hyundai-motor-group-innovation-center-singapore-set-to-transform-production%2C-r%26d-and-customer-experience-0000000363
168. BMW Group. (2023). *BMW group at NVIDIA GTC: Virtual production under way in future plant Debrecen.* BMW Group PressClub. Retrieved May 27, 2025, from https://www.press.bmwgroup.com/global/article/detail/T0411467EN/bmw-group-at-nvidia-gtc:-virtual-production-under-way-in-future-plant-debrecen
169. Attiko Metro, S. A. (2024). *The automatic system GoA4.* Thessaloniki Metro. Retrieved June 9, 2025, from https://www.thessmetro.gr/en/the-automatic-system-goa4/
170. RailTech. (2024). *NL: Driverless train 'successfully tested' on Dutch network.* RailTech.com. Retrieved May 27, 2025, from https://www.railtech.com/ertms/2024/12/09/ns-liet-trein-zonder-machinist-rijden-bij-groningen/
171. Roodt, D., Nadeem, M., & Vu, L. (2021). Managing complexity on digital systems: A model-based systems engineering approach. In *Conference on railway excellence (CORE 2021). Institution of railway signal engineers Australasia (IRSE Australasia).*
172. REWE Group. (2024). *On course for success with innovative technology: Three more REWE Pick&Go stores in Düsseldorf and Hamburg* [Online]. Retrieved May 27, 2025, from https://www.rewe-group.com/en/press-and-media/newsroom/press-releases/on-course-for-success-with-innovative-technology-three-more-rewe-pickgo-stores-in-dusseldorf-and-hamburg/
173. Loeb, W. (2024). *Amazon is removing just walk out technology.* Forbes. https://www.forbes.com/sites/walterloeb/2024/04/04/amazon-is-removing-just-walk-out-technology/
174. Ramsay, D. (2024). *Autonomous networks: Level 4 industry blueprint.* TM Forum. https://inform.tmforum.org/research-and-analysis/reports/autonomous-networks-level-4-industry-blueprint
175. Saunders, S. M. (2024). *Exclusive: World's first level 4 autonomous network makes comms history.* Fierce Network. https://www.fierce-network.com/modernization/exclusive-worlds-first-level-4-autonomous-network-makes-comms-history
176. Fisch, J. E., Labouré, M., & Turner, J. A. (2018). *The emergence of the Robo-advisor (PRC WP2018-12).* Pension Research Council, The Wharton School, University of Pennsylvania. Retrieved May 27, 2025, from https://pensionresearchcouncil.wharton.upenn.edu/wp-content/uploads/2018/12/WP-2018-12-Fisch-et-al.pdf

177. Feiler, L., Lütje, T., & Prokop, J. (2021). Robo-advice in wealth management: The German market. In *Banking business models* (pp. 167–189). Springer Gabler. https://doi.org/10.1007/978-3-658-33494-9_9
178. Marks&Spencer.(2024).*M&Sdrivescarbonreductionswithitsfirstautonomousfieldtrial*.Marks & Spencer Corporate Website. Retrieved May 27, 2025, from https://corporate.marksandspencer.com/media/press-releases/ms-drives-carbon-reductions-its-first-autonomous-field-trial
179. Ackerman, E. (2021). *What full autonomy means for the Waymo driver*. IEEE Spectrum Retrieved May 27, 2025, from https://spectrum.ieee.org/full-autonomy-waymo-driver
180. Davies, A. (2025). *Introducing Vulcan: Amazon's first robot with a sense of touch*. About Amazon. Retrieved May 27, 2025, from https://www.aboutamazon.com/news/operations/amazon-vulcan-robot-pick-stow-touch
181. Nokia. (2024). *Nokia AIMS boosts warehouse efficiency with industry-first, true automated inventory counting capability*. https://www.nokia.com/newsroom/nokia-aims-boosts-warehouse-efficiency-with-industry-first-true-automated-inventory-counting-capability
182. Cornet, H., & Gkemou, M. (Eds.). (2025). *Shared mobility revolution: Pioneering autonomous horizons* (Lecture notes in mobility). Springer. https://link.springer.com/book/10.1007/978-3-031-71793-2
183. Dong, X., DiScenna, M., & Guerra, E. (2019). Transit user perceptions of driverless buses. *Transportation, 46*, 35–50. https://link.springer.com/article/10.1007/s11116-017-9786-y
184. Wu, G., Li, D., Ding, H., Shi, D., & Han, B. (2024). An overview of developments and challenges for unmanned surface vehicle autonomous berthing. *Complex & Intelligent Systems, 10*, 981–1003. https://link.springer.com/content/pdf/10.1007/s40747-023-01196-z
185. Voudouris, C., Alsheddy, A., & Alhindi, A. (2025). Guided local search. In R. Martí, P. M. Pardalos, & M. G. Resende (Eds.), *Handbook of heuristics*. Springer. https://doi.org/10.1007/978-3-319-07153-4_2-2
186. Deloitte Insights. (2020). *Establishing a Centre of Excellence*. Retrieved May 27, 2025, from https://www2.deloitte.com/us/en/pages/operations/articles/center-of-excellence.html
187. Deloitte. (2023). *Is your AI center of excellence still a center of experimentation?* Retrieved May 27, 2025, from https://www2.deloitte.com/content/dam/Deloitte/us/Documents/consulting/us-is-your-ai-center-of-excellence-still-center-of-experimentation.pdf
188. Wade, M., Macaulay, J., Noronha, A., & Barbier, J. (2019). *Orchestrating transformation: How to deliver winning performance with a connected approach to change*. DBT Center Press.
189. Scheibenreif, D., Moyer, K., & Aykens, P.. (2018). *Four definitions make a digital business strategy process more effective*. Gartner Research Report G00352705, Gartner. Retrieved May 27, 2025, from https://www.gartner.com/document/3755764
190. Ant Group. (2025). *Technology*. Ant Group. Retrieved May 27, 2025, from https://www.antgroup.com/en/technology
191. Microsoft & LinkedIn. (2024). *2024 work trend index annual report*. Retrieved May 27, 2025, from https://assets-c4akfrf5b4d3f4b7.z01.azurefd.net/assets/2024/05/2024_Work_Trend_Index_Annual_Report_6_7_24_666b2e2fafceb.pdf
192. Enholm, I. M., et al. (2022). Artificial intelligence and business value: A literature review. *Information Systems Frontiers, 24*, 1709–1734. https://doi.org/10.1007/s10796-021-10186-w
193. Graham, L. (2024). *Sam Altman's one-person unicorn and the future of the office*. The Startup (Medium). Retrieved May 27, 2025, from https://medium.com/pi-labs-notes/sam-altmans-one-person-unicorn-and-the-future-of-the-office-8ca607b63012
194. Cooper, S. (2012). *Instagram's small workforce legitimizes other small start-ups*. Forbes. Retrieved May 27, 2025, from https://www.forbes.com/sites/stevecooper/2012/04/17/instagrams-small-workforce-legitimizes-other-small-start-ups/
195. AXELOS. (2019). *ITIL Foundation, ITIL 4 Edition*. The Stationery Office (TSO). ISBN: 9780113316168.
196. Kim, G., Humble, J., Debois, P., & Willis, J. (2016). *The DevOps handbook: How to create world-class agility, reliability, & security in technology organizations*. IT Revolution Press.

197. Atwal, H. (2020). *Practical DataOps: Delivering agile data science at scale*. Apress. https://doi.org/10.1007/978-1-4842-5104-1
198. Sabharwal, N., & Bhardwaj, G. (2022). *Hands-on AIOps: Best practices guide to implementing AIOps*. Apress. https://doi.org/10.1007/978-1-4842-8267-0
199. Shan, R., & Shan, T. (2025). Retrieval-augmented generation architecture framework: Harnessing the power of RAG. In R. Xu, H. Chen, Y. Wu, & L. J. Zhang (Eds.), *Cognitive computing - ICCC 2024. ICCC 2024* (Lecture notes in computer science) (Vol. 15426). Springer. https://doi.org/10.1007/978-3-031-77954-1_6
200. Pahune, S., & Akhtar, Z. (2025). Transitioning from MLOps to LLMOps: Navigating the unique challenges of large language models. *Information, 16*(2), 87. https://doi.org/10.3390/info16020087
201. Dong, L., Lu, Q., & Zhu, L. (2024). *A taxonomy of AgentOps for enabling observability of foundation model based agents*. arXiv preprint arXiv:2411.05285. https://arxiv.org/abs/2411.05285
202. Malik, S. (2025). *Introducing built-in AgentOps tools in Azure AI foundry agent service*. AI – Azure AI Services Blog, Microsoft Tech Community. Retrieved May 27, 2025, from https://techcommunity.microsoft.com/blog/azure-ai-services-blog/introducing-built-in-agentops-tools-in-azure-ai-foundry-agent-service/4414389
203. Gartner. (2024). *Gartner identifies the top 10 strategic technology trends for 2025*. Gartner. https://www.gartner.com/en/newsroom/press-releases/2024-10-21-gartner-identifies-the-top-10-strategic-technology-trends-for-2025
204. TM Forum. (2021). *Open digital architecture (ODA)*. TM Forum. https://www.tmforum.org/oda/
205. HR Open Standards Consortium. (2024). *HR Open Standards Framework*. HR Open Standards. https://www.hropenstandards.org
206. Bennett, M. (2013). The financial industry business ontology: Best practice for big data. *Journal of Banking Regulation, 14*, 255–268. https://doi.org/10.1057/jbr.2013.13
207. Dorne, R., & Voudouris, C. (2003). In M. G. C. Resende, J. Pinho, & C. de Sousa (Eds.), *HSF: The iOpt's framework to easily design meta-heuristic methods* (Metaheuristics: Computer decision-making) (Vol. 11, pp. 237–256). Combinatorial Optimization Book Series, Kluwer Academic Publishers.
208. Salesforce. (2024). *Agentforce guide: How to get started*. Salesforce. https://www.salesforce.com/agentforce/guide/
209. Microsoft. (2024). *Microsoft 365 Copilot Hub*. Microsoft Learn. https://learn.microsoft.com/en-us/copilot/microsoft-365/
210. SAP. (2024). *Joule Copilot from SAP*. SAP. https://www.sap.com/products/artificial-intelligence/ai-assistant.html
211. Wikipedia contributors. *Business process*. Wikipedia, The Free Encyclopedia. Retrieved May 27, 2025, from https://en.wikipedia.org/wiki/Business_process
212. Smith, D. (2021). *The cloud strategy cookbook*. Gartner. https://www.gartner.com/en/documents/3997036
213. Händler, T. (2023). *Balancing autonomy and alignment: A multi-dimensional taxonomy for autonomous LLM-powered multi-agent architectures*. arXiv preprint arXiv:2310.03659. https://arxiv.org/abs/2310.03659
214. Wikipedia contributors. (2024). *Business operating system (management)*. Wikipedia. https://en.wikipedia.org/wiki/Business_operating_system_(management)
215. Kerremans, M., & Robertson, B. (2016). *How a business operating system can guide CIOs to digital business success*. Gartner. https://www.gartner.com/en/documents/3467917
216. Wikipedia contributors. (2024). *SIPOC*. Wikipedia. https://en.wikipedia.org/wiki/SIPOC
217. Brown, C. (2018). Why and how to employ the SIPOC model. *Journal of Business Continuity & Emergency Planning, 12*(3), 199–208.
218. Reichheld, F. F. (2003). The one number you need to grow. *Harvard Business Review, 81*(12), 46–54.

219. Ding, W. (2022). Enterprise performance management optimization based on big data. In *Applications of decision science in management. Smart innovation, systems and technologies* (Vol. 260). Springer. https://link.springer.com/chapter/10.1007/978-981-19-2768-3_1
220. Kerremans, M., & Kopcho, J. (2019). *Create a digital twin of your organization to optimize your digital transformation program*. Gartner. https://www.gartner.com/en/documents/3901491
221. van der Aalst, W. M. P. (2022). Process mining: A 360 degree overview. In W. M. P. van der Aalst & J. Carmona (Eds.), *Process mining handbook* (Lecture notes in business information processing) (Vol. 448). Springer. https://doi.org/10.1007/978-3-031-08848-3_1
222. Ngo, M. T., Nguyen, N. H., Truong, C. D., Tran, D. H., & Truong, C. D. (2022). A proposed architecture of intelligent operations Center for smart cities development. In N. L. Anh, S. J. Koh, T. D. L. Nguyen, J. Lloret, & T. T. Nguyen (Eds.), *Intelligent systems and networks* (Lecture notes in networks and systems) (Vol. 471). Springer. https://doi.org/10.1007/978-981-19-3394-3_60
223. Wikipedia. (2024). *System of systems*. Wikipedia. https://en.wikipedia.org/wiki/System_of_systems
224. Lopes, S. D. S. (2025). *Risk management for system of systems: A systematic mapping study*. University of São Paulo. https://ieeexplore.ieee.org/document/9095601
225. Olivero, M. A., et al. (2024). A systematic mapping study on security for systems of systems. *International Journal of Information Security, 23*, 787–817. https://doi.org/10.1007/s10207-023-00757-0
226. Mitchell, M., Ghosh, A., Luccioni, A.S., & Pistilli, G. (2025). *Fully autonomous AI agents should not be developed*. arXiv preprint arXiv:2502.02649. https://arxiv.org/abs/2502.02649
227. Pope, A. (2024). *NYT v. OpenAI: The times's about-face*. Harvard Law Review Blog. https://harvardlawreview.org/blog/2024/04/nyt-v-openai-the-timess-about-face/
228. Patterson, D., Gonzalez, J., Le, Q., Liang, C., Munguia, L. M., Rothchild, D., So, D. R., Texier, M., & Dean, J. (2021). Carbon emissions and large neural network training. In *Proceedings of the 2021 ACM conference on equity and access in algorithms, mechanisms, and optimization* (pp. 1–7). ACM. https://doi.org/10.1145/3465416.3483307
229. Hao, K. (2024). *AI is taking water from the desert: New data centers are springing up every week. Can the earth sustain them?* The Atlantic. https://www.theatlantic.com/technology/archive/2024/03/ai-data-centers-water-use-arizona/677691/
230. Voudouris, C., & Gibbons, P. (2016). *Securing the digital railway* (Vol. Issue 227). IRSE News.
231. Firlej, M., & Taeihagh, A. (2020). Regulating human control over autonomous systems. *Regulation & Governance, 14*(3), 512–532. https://doi.org/10.1111/rego.12344
232. Christiano, P. F., Leike, J., Brown, T., Martic, M., Legg, S., & Amodei, D. (2017). Deep reinforcement learning from human preferences. In *Advances in neural information processing systems* (Vol. 30). https://arxiv.org/abs/1706.03741
233. Palumbo, G., Carneiro, D., & Alves, V. (2023). Observability: Towards ethical artificial intelligence. In *New trends in disruptive technologies, tech ethics and artificial intelligence (DiTTEt 2023), part of the advances in intelligent systems and computing series* (Vol. 1452). Springer.
234. United Nations. (2024). *Governing AI for humanity*. UN Advisory Body on Artificial Intelligence https://digitallibrary.un.org/record/4062495
235. OECD. (2024). *OECD AI principles*. Organisation for Economic Co-operation and Development. https://oecd.ai/en/ai-principles
236. G20. (2019). *G20 ministerial statement on trade and digital economy annex: G20 AI principles*. https://www.mofa.go.jp/policy/economy/g20_summit/osaka19/pdf/documents/en/annex_08.pdf
237. European Parliament. (2025). *EU AI act: First regulation on artificial intelligence*. European Union. https://www.europarl.europa.eu/pdfs/news/expert/2023/6/story/20230601STO93804/20230601STO93804_en.pdf

238. David, E. (2023). *Biden releases AI executive order directing agencies to develop safety guidelines.* The Verge. https://www.theverge.com/2023/10/30/23914507/biden-ai-executive-order-regulation-standards
239. Trump, D. J. (2025). Executive Order 14179: Removing barriers to American leadership in artificial intelligence. *Federal Register, 90*(20), 8741–8742. https://www.federalregister.gov/documents/2025/01/31/2025-02172/removing-barriers-to-american-leadership-in-artificial-intelligence
240. Cole, J., Sheng, M., & Leung, H. T. (2023). *New generative AI measures in China.* Ashurst. https://www.ashurst.com/en/insights/new-generative-ai-measures-in-china/
241. Ji, Y. (2025). *Manus: The first general AI agent from China.* Butterfly Effect. https://tech.co/news/manus-ai-everything-you-need-to-know
242. Ayres, I., & Balkin, J. M. (2024). The law of AI is the law of risky agents without intentions. *University of Chicago Law Review Online.* https://papers.ssrn.com/sol3/papers.cfm?abstract_id=4862025
243. Tully, S. (2024). *How to prevent millions of invisible law-free AI agents casually undermining the economy.* Fortune. https://fortune.com/2024/10/17/ai-agents-law-economy/
244. Bengio, Y., et al. (2023). *Statement on AI RISK. Center for AI Safety. A high-profile letter signed by leading AI researchers calling for a temporary pause in large-scale AI experiments.* https://www.safe.ai/statement-on-ai-risk
245. BBC Radio 4. (2023). *BBC inside science: AI and human extinction.* https://www.bbc.co.uk/programmes/m001md54
246. Bulletin of the Atomic Scientists. (2025). *Doomsday Clock.* https://thebulletin.org/doomsday-clock/
247. Wade, M. (2024). *IMD creates AI safety clock.* IMD Business School. https://www.imd.org/news/artificial-intelligence/imd-launches-ai-safety-clock/
248. Xiao, Y., Sun, E., Luo, D., & Wang, W. (2024). *TradingAgents: Multi-agents LLM financial trading framework.* arXiv preprint arXiv:2412.20138. https://arxiv.org/abs/2412.20138
249. Yang, R., Alayrac, J. B., & Altera Team. (2024). *Project Sid: Many-agent simulations toward AI civilization.* arXiv preprint arXiv:2411.00114. https://arxiv.org/abs/2411.00114
250. Luo, Y., Feng, Y., Xu, J., Tasca, P., & Liu, Y. (2025). *LLM-powered multi-agent system for automated crypto portfolio management.* arXiv preprint arXiv:2501.00826. https://arxiv.org/abs/2501.00826
251. Port of Rotterdam Authority. (2023). *Building the world's smartest port: Enabling autonomous navigation by 2030.* Port of Rotterdam Reports. https://www.portofrotterdam.com
252. Voudouris, C., Chernett, P., Wang, C. J., & Callaghan, V. (1995). Hierarchical behavioral control for autonomous vehicles. In *Proceedings of IFAC 2nd International Conference on Intelligent Autonomous Vehicles (IAV95)*, pp. 267–272. Helsinki University of Technology, Espoo, Finland, Elsevier Science.
253. Wang, Y., et al. (2024). *Scaling large motion models with million-level human motions.* arXiv preprint arXiv:2410.03311. https://arxiv.org/abs/2410.03311
254. Zhou, K., & Liu, Z. (2023). The promises and dangers of large vision models. *International Journal of Computer Vision, 131*, 1793–1795. https://doi.org/10.1007/s11263-023-01941-4
255. Voudouris, C., Chernett, P., Wang, C. J., & Callaghan, V. (1994). Fuzzy hierarchical control for autonomous vehicles. In *Proceedings of international symposium on intelligent robotics systems* (pp. 110–117).
256. Yee, L., Chui, M., Roberts, R., & Xu, S. (2024). *Why agents are the next frontier of generative AI.* McKinsey & Company. https://www.mckinsey.com/capabilities/mckinsey-digital/our-insights/why-agents-are-the-next-frontier-of-generative-ai
257. Loucks, J., Crossan, G., & Baris, B. (2025). *Autonomous generative AI agents: Under development.* Deloitte. https://www2.deloitte.com/us/en/insights/industry/technology/technology-media-and-telecom-predictions/2025/autonomous-generative-ai-agents-still-under-development.html

258. Capgemini Research Institute. (2024). *Harnessing the value of generative AI – 2nd Edition: Top use cases across sectors*. Capgemini. https://www.capgemini.com/wp-content/uploads/2024/05/Final-Web-Version-Report-Gen-AI-in-Organization-Refresh.pdf
259. Huang, J. (2025). *CES 2025 Keynote – The future of AI agents and enterprise IT*. NVIDIA Corporation, Consumer Electronics Show (CES). Retrieved June 15, 2025, from https://www.nvidia.com/en-us/events/ces/
260. Gupta, U. (2025). *Tech navigator: AgentOps and agentic lifecycle management*. Infosys Knowledge Institute. Retrieved June 15, 2025, from https://www.infosys.com/iki/research/agentops-agentic-lifecycle-management.html
261. Almeshaan, F., & Clarfield-Henry, A (2024). *AI agents and the future: The rise of ultra-generalists*. SmartBrief. Retrieved June 15, 2025, from https://www.smartbrief.com/original/ai-agents-and-the-future-the-rise-of-ultra-generalists
262. Yan, B., Zhang, X., Zhang, L., Zhang, L., Zhou, Z., Miao, D., & Li, C. (2025). *Beyond self-talk: A communication-centric survey of LLM-based multi-agent systems*. arXiv preprint arXiv:2502.14321. https://arxiv.org/abs/2502.14321
263. Hong, S., Zhuge, M., Chen, J., Zheng, X., Cheng, Y., Wang, J., Zhang, C., Wang, Z., Yau, S. K. S., Lin, Z., Zhou, L., Ran, C., Xiao, L., Wu, C., & Schmidhuber, J. (2024). MetaGPT: Meta programming for a multi-agent collaborative framework. In *International Conference on Learning Representations (ICLR) 2024*. arXiv preprint arXiv:2308.00352. https://arxiv.org/abs/2308.00352
264. Tesla. (2025). *Optimizing Optimus: 2025 All-hands update on humanoid robot production targets*. Internal Company Presentation. Retrieved June 15, 2025, from https://www.tesla.com/AI
265. Figure AI. (2024). *Figure 02 humanoid robot is ready to get to work*. The Robot Report. Retrieved June 15, 2025, from https://www.therobotreport.com/figure-02-humanoid-robot-is-ready-to-get-to-work/
266. Ha, H., Agrawal, S., & Song, S. (2021). Fit2Form: 3D Generative model for robot gripper form design. In *Proceedings of the 2020 Conference on Robot Learning (CoRL)*, Vol. 155, pp. 176–187. PMLR. Retrieved June 15, 2025, from https://proceedings.mlr.press/v155/ha21b.html
267. BMW Group, Figure AI. (2024). *BMW tests humanoid assembly robots from Figure AI at Spartanburg Plant*. Design News. Retrieved June 15, 2025, from https://www.designnews.com/automation/bmw-tests-humanoid-assembly-robots-figure-ai
268. Bolder Group. (2025). *The rise of AI agents in crypto*. Retrieved June 15, 2025, from https://boldergroup.com/insights/2025-the-rise-of-ai-agents-in-crypto/
269. Google. (2025). *Agent Development Kit: Easy to build multi-agent applications*. Google Developers Blog, 9 April 2025. Retrieved from https://developers.googleblog.com/en/agent-development-kit-easy-to-build-multi-agent-applications/
270. AGNTCY Project. (2025, March 6). Building the Internet of Agents: Introducing AGNTCY.org. *Outshift by Cisco (blog)*. Retrieved from https://outshift.cisco.com/blog/building-the-internet-of-agents-introducing-the-agntcy

www.ingramcontent.com/pod-product-compliance
Lightning Source LLC
Chambersburg PA
CBHW072359140925
32595CB00001B/4
9783032014146